B.

More Praise for *Awaken to Superconsciousness*:

"A Divine guide to inner and outer peace."
—Wayne Dyer, author of *Manifest Your Destiny*

"J. Donald Walters takes the great secrets of Yoga and meditation and makes them simple, practical, and understandable, accessible to the beginner, yet full of insight for the advanced seeker as well."
—Dr. David Frawley, author of *Ayurvedic Healing*

"This book will spark your inner light; reading it brings the tingle of awareness that always heralds peace and good things to come."
—*NAPRA Review*

"*Awaken to Superconsciousness* helps build the foundation so necessary to encounter difficult stages of your spiritual journey and daily life . . . it greatly widens the scope of Self-realization."
—Amrit Desai, author of
Kripalu Yoga: Meditation in Motion

"*Awaken to Superconsciousness* will stand out . . . . Much more than a book about meditation, it teaches the reader how to live in communion with God—blissfully, joyfully, and consciously."
—*Seattle New Times*

"J. Donald Walters imparts to us a lifetime of experience and knowledge about meditation. This book is compassionate, full of joy, and ultimately transforming."
—Stan Madson, Bodhi Tree Bookstore

AWAKEN TO
SUPERCONSCIOUSNESS

How to Use Meditation for Inner Peace,
Intuitive Guidance, and Greater Awareness

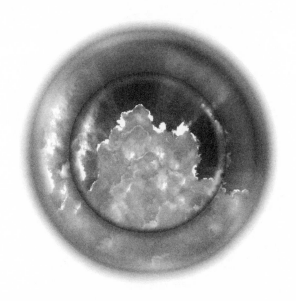

J. DONALD WALTERS

Cover and book design by C. A. Starner Schuppe
Cover photo and portrait of J. Donald Walters by C. A. Starner Schuppe

ISBN: 1-56589-136-8
Printed in the United States of America

3 5 7 9 10 8 6 4 2

This book was originally published as
Superconsciousness: A Guide to Meditation

Crystal

Clarity

Crystal Clarity, Publishers
14618 Tyler-Foote Road
Nevada City, CA 95959-8599

Phone: 800-424-1055 or 530-478-7600
Fax: 530-478-7610
E-mail: clarity@crystalclarity.com
Website: www.crystalclarity.com

Library of Congress Cataloging-in-Publication Data

Walters, J. Donald.
    [Superconsciousness]
    Awaken to Superconsciousness: how to use meditation for inner peace,
intuitive guidance, and greater awareness / J. Donald Walters
        p. cm.
    Originally published: Superconsciousness. New York: Warner Books,
1996.
    Includes bibliographical references and index.
    ISBN: 1-56589-136-8 (hardcover)
    1. Meditation. I. Title: Awaken to superconsciousness. II. Title.

BL627 .W35 2000
291.4'35—dc21
                                                        99-087361
                                                        CIP

CONTENTS

Introduction

I began meditating nearly fifty years ago, in 1948. Since then I haven't, to the best of my recollection, missed a single day of practice. No stern-minded self-discipline was needed to keep me regular. Meditation is simply the most meaningful activity in my life—indeed, the most meaningful activity I can imagine. I seriously wonder how people live without it. Meditation gives meaning to everything one does. As India's best-known scripture, the *Bhagavad Gita,* states, "To the peaceless person, how is happiness possible?" Inner peace is like lubricating oil: It enables the machinery of our lives to function smoothly. Without mental peace, our emotions, and the various demands placed upon us in our lives, grind together and create inner stress, leading eventually to some kind of physical or nervous breakdown.

Psychometric studies have shown that meditation produces a healthy ego, that it expands a person's world view and enables people to cope better with the stresses of life. Meditators, in addition, have shown significant gains in overcoming depression, neurotic behavior, and feelings of social inadequacy.

Meditation develops concentration, so essential for success in every activity. Often I have found, by meditation-induced concentration, that I can accomplish in an afternoon what others have required days or even weeks to complete. In three days, some years ago, I wrote melodies for eighteen of Shakespeare's lyrics; in a single day, more recently, twenty-one of the thirty-three melodies for my oratorio, *Christ Lives,* which has had hundreds of performances in America and in Europe. In one day, recently, I wrote thirty-one melodies for an audiotape of my mini-book *Secrets of Happiness;* and in one day also, my entire book *Do It NOW!,* which has a different saying for every day of the year. (I did need a month, later, to edit the book for publication.)

Before taking up meditation, I would sometimes stare at a page for days before I could write down a single word. Even then, I doubted whether what I'd written was what I really wanted to say.

Inspiration, which many highly creative people consider out of their hands, can be summoned *at will* by one-pointed concentration, and by magnetizing the flow of thoughts and ideas in meditation.

Physical fatigue can be banished also, by putting ourselves in tune with inner abundance, flowing to us from infinity. The deeper this attunement, through meditation, the greater the abundance we experience in every aspect of our lives.

It was from a great master of yoga, Paramhansa Yogananda, that I learned the art and science of meditation. I read his *Autobiography of a Yogi*[*] in 1948, and was so moved by it that I took the next bus from New York City to Los Angeles, where he had his headquarters. The day I met him, he accepted me as a disciple, and I lived with him as a monk for the remaining three and a half years of his life. I have been his disciple ever since.

[*]At that time published by Philosophical Library, New York; later, by Self-Realization Fellowship, Los Angeles. Recently, the first edition has been reprinted by Crystal Clarity, Publishers, Nevada City, CA 95959, which also publishes most of my books.

The path of yoga that he taught was not that of the physical postures of *hatha yoga,* but the ancient meditative path of *raja yoga.* Of *raja yoga,* the highest technique, mentioned in several places in his autobiography, is *kriya yoga.* This present volume is based on the ancient *raja yoga* traditions and on his teachings. It serves as a preparation also for *kriya yoga* initiation. My own spiritual name, by which I am known in many spiritual circles, is Kriyananda, meaning "divine bliss through *kriya yoga.*"

The teachings of *raja yoga* are the best guide to meditation that I know. They are completely non-sectarian, and can be practiced with equal effectiveness by anyone regardless of that person's religious affiliation or lack of affiliation. The goal of these teachings is superconscious realization: the realization of who and what you are in your highest, spiritual reality. It is, as you can see, a very personal goal for each seeker. I have therefore tried to explain it in a spirit of humble respect for your own deepest spiritual needs.

This book is for several audiences.

First, it is for the beginning meditator that wants an east-to-follow, self-consistent system based not on scholarship or on desultory reading, but on the practical experience of a great master, supplemented by my own personal practice and experience.

Second, I've written for experienced meditators, to bring them to a new and deeper level in their practice, and to offer them helpful pointers as well as answers to problems they may have encountered during their own practices.

Third, this book is for people who are on other spiritual paths but don't realize the importance of direct spiritual experience. As Paramhansa Yogananda put it, "Meditation is to religion what the laboratory is to science."

Fourth, this book is for people generally who, without necessarily realizing it, seek deeper meaning in life.

Fifth and finally, this book is for those who, while not ready to take up meditation, desire deeper understanding of the phenomenon of consciousness.

I have aimed to make this book as deep, and at the same time as clear, simple, comprehensive, and enjoyable to read, as possible.

I am aware that some readers prefer to omit God from any effort at self-improvement, including the practice of meditation. I show in this book that, without aspiration toward some higher reality, one is left meandering mentally in a labyrinth. Whether you call that higher reality God, Cosmic Intelligence, or your own higher Self, it is infinitely above your normal waking state of awareness.

I refer to God as "He" for the reason that, in English (as in many other languages), the masculine pronoun is also the impersonal. Something precious would be lost if we referred to the Godhead as It. For though God has no gender, God is not a thing. God is conscious; God knows us; God *loves* us. But one cannot keep on saying "God . . ." this and "God . . ." that without giving the impression that one is clumping about on stilts in an iris bed. Any attempt to be exact in one's references to God is almost laughable: How can the human mind even begin to grasp Infinity?

My practice has been, when referring to human beings as individuals, to use the impersonal pronoun, "he," in cases where my reference is to the forever-sexless soul encased in a human body. "It" obviously wouldn't do. To follow the modern convention of saying "he/she" would be stylistically cumbersome, and (worse still) would force the reader's attention to a lower level by emphasizing superficial and spiritually non-essential differences.

PART I

DIVINE MEMORY

Chapter One

SUPERCONSCIOUSNESS: THE CENTRAL REALITY

Consciousness, in its pure state, is absolute: more absolute than the speed of light, which slows on entering a material medium such as the earth's atmosphere; more absolute than the existence of matter, which is only a manifestation of energy; more absolute than energy, which is itself a vibration of consciousness.

We've been taught to think of consciousness as the product of brain activity. To Descartes, this activity was the final proof of existence. "I think," he wrote, "therefore I am." He was mistaken. It isn't thought that produces awareness. It is awareness that produces thought. It takes consciousness to think. We are not *less* aware when we aren't thinking, nor *more* aware when our brains are very active. Many people have experienced moments of intense awareness, and have discovered at those times that their minds were more than ordinarily still. I can't imagine this degree of awareness in a restless mind.

It is possible to increase the frequency and intensity of this experience, which gives us glimpses of a potential we all have within us: a state of heightened awareness known as superconsciousness. The method for achieving this state will be the subject of this book. As we proceed, you will learn how to become wholly free of thought, yet more fully aware than you've ever been. You will learn, with awareness of your higher Self, how to achieve perfect love, ineffable joy, and calm, self-expansive wisdom.

Descartes's explanation was the product of an essentially Western bias: that rational thought is the best, if not the only, key to understanding. Since the time of the Greeks this bias has been firmly entrenched. And because of it, it is not surprising that scientists nowadays view computers, and the similarities between them and the way the brain works, as evidence that consciousness itself is the product of computer-like activity in the brain. They define thought as a pattern of electrons, merely, moving through a circuit of brain cells. Materialists—their own electrons moving smugly through this particular circuitry!—fasten in grim triumph on that word, "merely." How, they ask, proud of their objectivity, can one avoid the conclusion that no one is really conscious at all? As a KGB interrogator is said to have told a young woman he was torturing for information, "You are no more conscious than that concrete wall over there."

Suppose a computer were asked to reproduce, by a random selection of words, some great work of literature, such as the Bible. Conceivably, after a few billion, trillion, or zillion tries it might get all of the words right, and in the right sequence. But the result would have no more literary value than random patterns of clouds in the sky, which may fleetingly resemble mountain ranges, houses, or human faces before moving on to assume other shapes. Because there would be no conscious person directing the computer's selection of words, the process would continue haphazardly, losing in an instant its brief resemblance to scripture.

The only way for this process to become meaningful would be for someone *consciously* to recognize what the computer had done and to stop the process in time.

Consciousness, in other words, is not the *product* of brain activity: It is the fundamental reality without which thinking as a conscious activity could never take place.

POTENTIALITY VS. ACTUALITY

There is another approach to this question of consciousness as a phenomenon that exists outside the physical brain. If a thing is potentially real, that potentiality must be considered in its own way actual also. Nothing could appear in actuality that didn't exist already as a potential. No melody could be written that wasn't there already to be written. No mountain could be climbed if the potential didn't already exist in the human body to accomplish that feat. And life itself could not have appeared on this planet were life not a potential from the planet's very beginnings.

Science speaks of two kinds of energy: potential and kinetic. Were it not for the potential energy in a pendulum, for example, prior to its downward swing, there would be no downward swing, and therefore no kinetic energy. A lizard, similarly, could never write a Shakespearean drama, nor a cow act the role of Juliet: They simply haven't the *potential*.

The fact that consciousness ever appeared on the stage of time means that it was there backstage, awaiting its cue, from the very beginning, when galactic gases were still coalescing and forming molten rock. The same must be said of life: The fact that life appeared means that it always had the potential to appear, which is one way of saying that, in some form, it always existed.*

Biologists have gone to great lengths to show that life and consciousness evolved by a process of purely random, accidental, and purposeless selection. What can one call their patient labor but a most impressive exercise in futility? The very appearance of life and consciousness means that both must have been present in latent form even before the Big Bang, or whatever it was that raised the curtain on the cosmic drama.

Materialism posits matter as the ultimate reality. Physicists demolished this concept early in the twentieth century when they discovered that matter is only a manifestation of energy. But materialists soon recovered from that seeming deathblow to their philosophy. They simply re-named the ultimate reality "energy." Anything, for them, would fit the bill as long as it didn't demolish their claim that consciousness is the product, not the cause, of material manifestation.

Physicists, meanwhile, have been joining the metaphysicians in growing numbers in their belief that

*I have argued these points at length in my book *Crises in Modern Thought*, Crystal Clarity, Publishers, Nevada City, CA 95959.

18

consciousness is not the product of anything, but is itself the Ultimate Cause.

Consciousness works *through* the brain, but doesn't require a brain to exist. It was, indeed, consciousness that produced the brain, as it did everything else in existence—even the apparently insensate rocks.

J. C. Bose, the great Indian scientist, in testing the response of living and "non-living" matter to a wide variety of stimuli, demonstrated early in the twentieth century that there is essentially no difference in response between nerve tissues and metals. Other tests were conducted decades later, with virtually identical results, by the great German physicist Karl Bonhoefer.

These demonstrations suggest only two possible alternatives: Either *nothing* is conscious (an absurdity, considering our interest in the subject), or consciousness is inherent in all things.

Consciousness requires a material medium, such as the brain, to bring it into material manifestation, but it requires no such medium, to exist. The outward manifestation of consciousness was a potential from the beginning of creation. That this is not an inference, but an actual fact, can be experienced in superconsciousness by anyone who attains deep states of meditation. As the *Bhagavad Gita,* India's best-known scripture, states, that essential consciousness exists everywhere, but is forever unaffected by anything.

The universality of consciousness helps to explain a scientific anomaly. Telepathy, so often demonstrated as to be held no longer in serious doubt, continues to baffle researchers because, unlike that of any other known phenomenon, the power of thought remains constant with increasing distance. Every other known force, including light, diminishes with distance, but a thought can be received as clearly on the other side of the earth as in the next room.

Superconsciousness takes human awareness outside the brain. We may say even that the brain is only a filter for superconsciousness. It can serve as a window onto superconsciousness, much as windows themselves reveal the scenery lying beyond them, but the brain can no more *produce* superconsciousness than a window can produce scenery.

That is why scientists encounter so much frustration in their efforts to subject higher levels of awareness to testing by the scientific method. The conscious mind cannot oblige superconsciousness to do its bidding, any more than Alice in Wonderland could oblige her croquet ball, which was a hedgehog, to remain wherever she placed it. The conscious mind, including the reasoning faculty, is subordinate to superconsciousness, not superior to it.

Consciousness existed before the appearance of matter—before the appearance even of time and space. In this context, Pure Consciousness is not really even *omnipresent:* It simply *is*. It was vibrations of that consciousness that produced energy, and then, through grosser vibrations of energy, produced matter. Without these movements of consciousness, time and space wouldn't exist. The very finitude of space, claimed as a fact by physicists, is acceptable to the mind only if one thinks of the universe as a vast idea. For thought alone can so circumscribe itself that nothing, literally, exists outside it.

Years ago in India I invited a great saint, Anandamoyee Ma, to visit America. "I am there already" was her reply. To her, in her state of superconscious awareness, material limitations were non-existent. She was as much conscious of being in America as in her own physical body in India.

My guru, Paramhansa Yogananda, put it to me this way: "It is an effort for me, in this superconscious state, to remember which body I am supposed to keep moving. I am present in *all* bodies!" One day he told someone, "You have a sour taste in your mouth, haven't you?" "How did you know?" the other asked in surprise. "Because I am as much in your body as I am in my own," the master replied.

As consciousness projects itself into the material universe, it takes on not only material forms, but also the *qualities* manifested by those forms. In the rocks, it becomes rocklike. In the flowers and trees, it takes on a limited degree of outward movement, and, with movement, a suggestion of dreamlike awareness. In the animals it expresses greater movement, and also greater awareness. In more highly evolved animals, it manifests a degree of intelligence, primarily instinctual.

The Human Potential

Only in mankind does consciousness reveal its potential for abandoning its material identity altogether. The fact that human beings seem to possess a capacity for increasing their awareness indefinitely suggests that they may even have the potential to continue that expansion to infinity.

Rational thought suggests, and the experience of great mystics—the "scientists" of the spiritual world—confirms, that human beings, with their more highly refined nervous system, have the potential to transcend ego-awareness altogether, and attain cosmic consciousness. For the purposes of this book I have called that universal state superconsciousness, though, to be exact, superconsciousness is but a rung on the ladder to cosmic consciousness.

Paramhansa Yogananda, in *Autobiography of a Yogi,*[*] described divine vision as "center everywhere, circumference nowhere." As consciousness moves outward from its center into material manifestation, it takes on the appearance of material limitation.

In human beings, too, superconsciousness is filtered as if through heavy, smoked glass. It is not possible for people to achieve perfection outwardly, since any outward flow of energy and attention only continues the process of filtration. We can attain perfection only by reversing our flow of energy and consciousness from the objective world, as it is revealed to us by our senses, and directing it inward to our divine center.

This is the essence of all true spiritual teaching. Outer practices and beliefs are helpful only to the extent that they inspire us to seek our divine center within. This is what Jesus Christ meant by his statement "The kingdom of God is within you" (Luke 17:21).

The secret of self-transcendence is daily, deep meditation.

---

[*]Chapter 22, p. 205 of the first edition, which is cited throughout.

****

MEDITATION PRACTICE

Plumb the depths of intuitive perception within you, at the calm center of your own heart. If any restless or disturbing feelings arise there, withdraw deeper still— to the very center of feeling, as if to the calm eye of a storm. As any period on this page might be reduced indefinitely in size, even to the point of becoming invisible under the strongest microscope, without ever ceasing to exist, so there is no limit to how deeply you can withdraw into the center of your being.

Try to find the innermost center of intuitive perception in your heart. If you experience the slightest disturbance, go deeper still. Finally you will enter a vast hall of calmness.

That center is the center of everything, everywhere. This, not intellectual analysis, is the way to attain perfect insight into people and events—into any difficulty that you face in life. This is the way of intuitive understanding. Your intuition must be cultivated—not abstractly, but with kindness toward all, with acceptance of whatever happens, and with perfect love for all life.

This is also the way to banish pain, both physical and emotional. Focus with calm feeling on your inner center, then project that center into the pain; visualize yourself at its center, and concentrate there. If you can penetrate deeply enough to its center, it will cease to exist. You will find, then, an ability to cope with any trauma. When you can understand everything from its center, you will find that you can turn even major set-backs in your life to good advantage.

Similarly, when faced with any problem in life, or when undertaking creative projects, or to help you attune yourself to countless situations: Seek your own heart center; then from that center visualize the center of the matter at hand. You will know, suddenly, exactly what to do.

It is more difficult to visualize the center of an abstraction, such as a problem. Think of your definitions of it, then, as layers to be peeled off and cast away. When no layers remain, you will find yourself at its center. To clarify your intuitive awareness at that center, hold that awareness up to superconsciousness.

By this practice, you will find everything you do to be increasingly appropriate, uniquely so for that moment, and always different from anything else you've ever done.

Chapter Two

Raising Your Consciousness

One often hears references to "altered states of consciousness." Implied in the expression is a suggestion that higher states of awareness are anomalies.

Actually, there is only one state of consciousness: superconsciousness. The conscious and subconscious minds are our "altered states," representing as they do the downward filtering of superconsciousness through the brain. Superconsciousness is, forever, the reality. It is our true and native state of being.

The secret of meditation, then, lies not in affirming states that are foreign to us, but in reclaiming what we *are*. Meditation is a returning to our center within. It may be termed a process of upward relaxation into superconsciousness. The only "effort" required is to resist the tendency, born of habit, toward tension and restlessness. What we must do, simply, is increase our receptivity—mentally and emotionally first, and then intuitively.

THE BEST POSTURE

For perfect relaxation, one might expect the best position to be stretched out flat on one's back. This may be true for physical relaxation, but not for superconsciousness. In meditation, it is important to sit upright, with a straight spine. A supine position induces a passive state of mind, even sleep.

Here are a few affirmations to use just prior to meditating, each accompanied by brisk physical movement to strengthen the impact of the words on your mind:

1) Walk vigorously in place before meditating. Affirm, "I am awake and ready! I am awake and ready!"

2) Extend your arms vigorously out to the side, then in front, then high above the head, affirming, "I am positive! energetic! enthusiastic!" a) Begin with your hands at the chest, flinging your arms out to the side with the affirmation, "I am positive!" b) Bring the hands back to the chest, then extend the arms vigorously in front of you with the affirmation, "energetic!" c) Bring the hands back again to the chest, then fling them high above your head with the affirmation, "enthusiastic!" d) Finally, relax the arms at the side. Repeat this exercise and affirmation several times, as you like.

3) Rap your knuckles lightly on the forearms and upper arms, first with the right fist, then with the left, affirming, "I am master of my body! I am master of myself!" Repeat this exercise several times.

4) Rub your arms, legs, hips, chest, and other parts of the body while affirming, "Awake! Rejoice, my body cells!"

5) Rap your scalp lightly with your knuckles, affirming, "Be glad, my brain! Be wise and strong!"

6) Massage your scalp lightly all over with the fingertips, affirming, "Awake, my sleeping children! Wake!"

Meditation isn't a matter of waiting passively for something to happen. Whatever higher awareness, inspiration, or guidance you receive, participate in the experience with calm, *committed* awareness. For you will never attain superconsciously inspired experiences except on their own level of intense awareness.

Subconsciousness lies, as the word implies, *below* the level of conscious awareness. Its physical seat in the body is the lower brain and the spine. The more our energy and awareness are uplifted in the spine and projected forward through the brain toward the frontal lobe, the higher our level of awareness will be. Concentrate in the frontal lobe of the brain, at a point midway between the eyebrows.

The spine is the tunnel through which consciousness ascends to enlightenment. It begins from the dimmest awareness at the base of the spine, and ends at the seat of superconsciousness between the eyebrows. In animals, and (less so) in animalistic human beings, the energy and consciousness are centered in the lower part of the spine and in the lower brain.

It is interesting to note that dogs express pleasure by wagging their tails. That is because pleasure energizes them at their normal center of awareness in the lower spine. The tail itself is a downward extension of the spine, and indicates downwardness as the basic direction of their energy and consciousness. When a dog is fearful or dispirited, it shows a loss of energy through an accentuation of that downward movement, by curling its tail between its legs, and even by curving its lower spine downward.

Human beings, whom the process of evolution has raised to higher levels of awareness, show pleasure more in the upper part of their bodies, by smiling—even, sometimes (in this sense affording an amusing contrast to our canine friends!), by wagging their heads. Other gestures indicate an upward flow of energy. They sit up straight, throw out their chests, walk lightly on their feet, look upward.

I remember once seeing in a pharmacy window a print of a painting depicting a young man dreaming of the glorious future before him as a pharmacist. He was looking upward, naturally. It would have given another message altogether had he been portrayed looking down. For people look down when they feel badly, or at least when they withdraw into themselves. When they feel really badly, they slump forward; their chests cave inward; the corners of their mouths curve downward in a pout.

Little children, who are less inhibited about letting their bodies express what they feel, jump up and down when they are happy, as if wishing they could fly. When they are unhappy, on the other hand, they stamp their feet angrily, even let gravity pull them to the floor, where they lie screaming, or in other ways reveal the downward movement of their consciousness and energy.

Heaven and Hell Lie within Us

Heaven, in every religion, is described as being somewhere "up above." Hell is located somewhere "down below." There is no objective evidence for either belief. No telescope has revealed, nor has any space probe discovered, green pastures and bands of singing angels. Nor have oil gushers brought up protesting hordes of imps and devils.

As a child I theorized that heaven was located on Saturn because of its rings, which I imagined must be its halo. My theory broke down, however, when I learned that Saturn was just as often below me relative to my position on Earth. My belief in heaven itself suffered a major setback when I learned that what was "up" for me was "down" for people on the other side of the world— that, in a cosmic sense, up and down don't even exist. One might even say that, in that sense, we don't really know whether we're coming or going.

Yet there *is* one absolute direction. Science tells us that the universe, *in relation to itself,* is expanding. By the same token our consciousness, too, *in relation to itself,* expands or contracts. As our consciousness and sympathies expand, our center of energy, like a helium balloon, rises. With contraction, that center of energy, like a deflating balloon, descends.

It is a universal experience that pure love and other heavenly feelings are accompanied by an upward flow of energy, and that any hell we experience on earth is accompanied by a downward flow. When we feel happy, our consciousness rises. When we feel unhappy, it sinks. Language itself takes universal cognizance of this fact.

29

In English we say "I feel uplifted" or "I feel high." If we feel badly we say, "I feel downcast" or "I feel low." There are comparable expressions in other languages. (In Italian, for example, people say, *"Mi sento giu oggi"*—"I feel low today.")

Heaven and hell have no outward location. They are directions of energy and consciousness in ourselves. They are "above" us or "below" us relative to the higher or lower centers of consciousness in our own bodies.

Hell represents the lower centers of consciousness in the spine—those states of relative unawareness from which humanity has risen in its long evolutionary climb. Heaven represents the higher centers of consciousness; the highest heaven is that level of perfect awareness which is superconsciousness.

All life is impelled up the spiral staircase of the spine by a kind of soul memory. Invertebrates, having no such staircase themselves, can only stand at the bottom, so to speak, looking up. But with the appearance of the spine in evolution, a tunnel forms through which energy and consciousness can rise. The higher we rise within ourselves, the closer we come to heaven within ourselves.

This increasing freedom of consciousness gives us the freedom of choice to move upward or downward. If our old materialistic habits trick us into taking the downward direction, we find ourselves once again living in relative unawareness. Because of the contrast between that lessened awareness and our higher awareness of recent memory, that decreased awareness becomes for us an inner hell of depression, loneliness, and despair.

One would think that, since what everyone wants is happiness, everyone would choose to move upward, into the higher centers of the spine. Unfortunately, the matter is not quite so easy as simply deciding on a direction and behaving accordingly. Habit is a powerful influence. In addition, wherever energy is centered, there is a focus for a certain amount of pleasure. Because of the pain of a mosquito sting, energy is drawn to that spot. There is not only pain, but also a certain amount of pleasure in scratching it.

Long association with matter has conditioned us to consider our bodies our true identity. The body, however, is merely a filter through which the higher Self expresses itself on this material plane. All life is drawn into the upward spiral of evolution by the silent call of the Self.

Human beings especially are aware, though most of them only dimly so, of how persistent that call is to ascend to higher levels of consciousness. The call is usually drowned out by the seemingly more immediate and pressing demands of outer life. One recalls the prayer of St. Augustine, "Lord, make me good, but not yet!"

We live in a state of constant conflict between our higher and our lower natures. Somehow we carry deep within us the dim, ancient memory of our higher nature, but the lower represents for us the security of the familiar. It is this sense of ego-familiarity, rather than soul-remembrance, that draws us downward into diminished awareness; this fact, however, doesn't always represent to our minds the disaster it actually is, for we imagine it as a comfortable alternative to meeting life's challenges head on. Wouldn't it be easier, we wonder, simply to let ourselves become less aware?

There is the call to soul-freedom in higher awareness, and the opposing call to a delusive freedom in unawareness: the call of the sacred, and of the profane.

LEVELS OF REFINEMENT:

THE "PEASANT" TYPE

The refinement of the human ego is as gradual as the upward climb of evolution itself. People whose reality is wholly identified with their physical bodies still have a long climb ahead of them. Only dimly aware, as yet, of how priceless is the gift of human intelligence and of its potential for creative action, they live in mere reaction to sense stimuli, as the animals do. Such people are problem-oriented, not solution-oriented, by nature. In response to any challenge, if they can't combat it on a level of muscle or emotion, they are likely to develop victim consciousness. Their sense of right and wrong is determined by their habit patterns and by the opinions of others, never by deep inner conviction.

People fall into universal categories of refinement. Such people as these may be classed as peasant types. In social standing, they may fall into any category. They may be aristocrats or millionaires. Many real peasants don't fit the type at all. Peasant types, then, not necessarily peasants by social position, are passively subservient to circumstances, and to the will of others. Generally speaking, they let other people do their thinking for them. Success and failure are comprehensible to them only in terms of pleasure and pain.

The peasant type is not chiseled in stone, but covers a gradation of development that might be compared to the first flight on a long upward staircase. The ego, as it mounts toward the top of this first flight, becomes increasingly aware that more can be accomplished by intelligence than by muscle alone.

THE MERCHANT TYPE

The climb up the second flight involves a steady increase in the use of intelligence. The level of refinement on this second flight is not yet as to bestow an *expansion* of intelligent awareness. Intelligence is used, rather, for selfish gain. The goal is personal advancement, and the brain is used schemingly toward that end. Right and wrong are determined by the question "What's in it for me?" Success or failure are defined in terms of winning, or not winning, over the opposition.

Such people have what may be described as merchant consciousness, for theirs is a ceaseless search for personal advantage. There are many merchants in real life, of course, who don't display these characteristics, as well as many in other walks who display them to a T. Merchant consciousness, then, simply epitomizes a stage in the process of human development where the ego uses its human intelligence not for the attainment of wisdom, but cunningly, for self-serving ends. Such people take for granted that everyone is so motivated. They laugh at the thought that anyone would do anything from altruistic motives. "Everyone," they say mockingly, "has his price."

This second flight of stairs, too, has its gradations, from the unscrupulous con man to the wealthy man or woman who donates to charities in order to gain admiration and respect in the eyes of the world. The person who helps others, even from selfish motives, discovers in the act of giving more satisfaction than he ever felt in being merely important. In the first state he was envied; in the second he is loved.

Thus, gradually, his sympathies expand to include in his self-interest the interests of others.

THE SELF-OFFERING, WARRIOR TYPE

The ego arrives at the third flight of stairs when it begins to find its limited identification with the ego no longer natural, but stifling. Now it dreams of expanding its identity to include in its own happiness the happiness of an increasing number of others; to embrace ever-broader horizons in its sphere of awareness.

The self-expansive ego thinks in terms of serving rather than of being served; of self-sacrifice for the good of many rather than of sacrificing others for its own good. It sees right and wrong, now, as abstract principles; success or failure, as the ability or inability to live up to those principles.

The epitome of this attitude is that of the warrior, or of the selfless political leader—a person willing, in other words, to give his or her very life for the general good. Ideally, this type of person is noble and self-giving.

Obviously, it doesn't describe the only, or even the typical, warrior or political leader as we've come to know them. Many people in such roles today are self-serving and aggressive. There are also countless people in other walks of life whose greatest joy lies in helping others. This third flight of stairs, then, may be named the warrior category for the sake of simplicity. It describes a type of human being, not a social function. None of these categories should be taken as a rule for limiting people. They only point out a general direction for our own spiritual development.

The closer the ego approaches to the top of this third flight of stairs, the more clearly it begins to realize that even noble deeds are self-limiting if they proceed from ego-consciousness. "How much good," it asks, "can I really accomplish on my own?"

The Priestly, God-Seeking Type

When human evolution reaches the fourth level of development, the ego conceives the desire to be guided solely by superconsciousness. The higher it mounts this fourth flight of stairs, the more keenly it desires to attain those states of consciousness which are mankind's highest potential. Thus, the longing grows within, first to commune with, and then to become united with, the vastness of superconsciousness.

Eventually, there blossoms in the mind a perception of life's oneness, and a desire to awaken all humanity to the understanding that there is only one goal in life: oneness with God.

Ideally, the epitome of this fourth stage is the priest, or spiritual teacher. It includes all, however, who deeply aspire to unite their souls with God.

THE SPINE AS A MAGNET

The pathway of spiritual attainment is the spine. This pathway may be compared to a bar magnet, the molecules of which are aligned north and south. The larger the number so aligned, the stronger the magnetism in that bar of steel. In human beings, the more the energy in the spine is directed up toward the brain, the stronger is its own magnetism. If the magnetism is strong, these people can attract to themselves all good things, including the more subtle benefits of spiritual insight and understanding.

Magnetism in physics is also generated by an electric current. The stronger the current, the stronger the magnetic field. The flow of energy in the spine, similarly, generates a magnetic field—animal, or spiritual, depending on the quality of consciousness behind that energy. This power functions on much the same principle as electro-magnetism, but is, in its own way, far more powerful. As the strength of electromagnetism depends on the strength of the electric current, so our personal magnetism depends on the strength of our will, the determinant also of the strength of our energy-flow.

The stronger our magnetism, the more infallibly we attract to ourselves whatever it is we seek in life. As cosmic energy is a vibration of divine consciousness, so our bodily energy, and the energy we project into the world around us, is the projection of our human will. The stronger that will, the greater also will be the flow of energy. Consequently, the greater also will be our magnetic field.

As a person evolves spiritually, it becomes vitally important for him to harbor thoughts that are benign and uplifting. For by negative thinking he may attract to himself, and to others, the very things he fears for himself and them.

MEDITATION IS FOR ALL

Meditation is the best way to speed up the process of spiritual evolution, regardless of the stage a person has reached on the long staircase to enlightenment. Even those on the "first flight" can benefit from meditation, though the more likely time for taking up meditative practices is on the "third flight," that of ego-expansiveness. The *Bhagavad Gita* states, "By steadfast meditation on Me, even the worst of sinners speedily comes to Me."

Meditation is, as I have said, a process of ever deeper relaxation. We usually think of relaxation as a sinking downward into passivity and sleep. There is, however, a higher kind of relaxation, which involves a response to the call of the soul. The more consciously we respond to that call, by meditating and offering up our hearts' devotion, the more we find ourselves relaxing, not downward into subconsciousness, but *upward* into superconsciousness, drawn there by the "gravitational" pull of divine grace.

It was to clarify this higher call that the caste system evolved in India. For centuries, that system has been abused by human egoism and ignorance; ultimately it has become an ironclad system for perpetuating the abuse. Originally, however, it was intended to encourage human beings in the direction of their own enlightenment. It was not meant to be hereditary. The *sudra* (peasant), *vaisya* (merchant), *kshatriya* (warrior, or political leader), and *brahmin* (priest) were simply levels of spiritual development. As the Indian scriptures state, "A *brahmin* is not truly a *brahmin* unless he lives in the consciousness of a *brahmin*."

REINCARNATION AS A NECESSITY
FOR HUMAN DEVELOPMENT

Once we see an actual direction in human development, we see in it also a rationale for the doctrine of reincarnation that cannot but appeal to anyone's sense of the fitness of things. For so long as people imagine reincarnation to be a doctrine with no rhyme or reason, it is easy to dismiss the whole thing as an interesting, but somewhat unattractive, superstition. The way reincarnation has often been explained, life seems to be a sort of lottery. If the numbers are against us, they can cause us to be born as spiders or flies, or as anything at all. Who could take such a system seriously? But if there is a direction to human evolution, and especially if evolution can take us to the heights of consciousness, then it seems obvious that more than one life is needed to complete an ongoing process that we see happening around us all the time.

Whatever level you have attained, yourself, in your spiritual evolution, you can progress more rapidly if, in meditation, you direct your energies and consciousness up the spine, and expand them outward from the ego to include the happiness of all in your own happiness.

Jesus Christ said it all when, quoting the scriptures, he stated, "Thou shalt love the Lord thy God with all thy heart, and with all thy soul, and with all thy strength [a reference to energy], and with all thy mind; and thy neighbor as thyself" (Luke 10:27).

Meditation is the highway to this state of perfect enlightenment.

****

A MEDITATION EXERCISE

Sit upright, keeping your spine straight and your body relaxed. To relax completely, first inhale deeply and tense the whole body. Next, exhale forcibly and relax. Repeat this exercise two or three times.

Now, holding your body very still, think of your skin as the outer crust of our planet Earth. Within this crust is contained everything. The earth's rivers are the blood coursing through your veins. The oceans with their mighty tides are your lungs. The woods and forests are the hairs on your head and on the skin of your body. The plains are the broad expanses of your back and abdomen. The humble receptivity of the valleys is expressed in the upturned palms of your hands. The hills and mountains are your shoulders and cranium. The wind blowing over the earth is your breath. God's love for all the world radiates outward like a light from your own heart.

Send love outward in blessing to all humanity, to all creatures, to all things, moving and unmoving, everywhere.

Chapter Three

STILLING THE WAVES

Meditation has much in common with science. Both strive for objectivity, and both depend—far more than most scientists realize—on intuition. Moreover, though meditation takes one beyond logic, it cannot do so if it ignores the reasonable checks of common sense.

The German philosopher Hegel stated the creed of rationalism in these words: "All that is real is rational, and all that is rational is real." The fundamental hope of rationalism is that by seeing the reason behind things you will understand them and, with that understanding, be able to control everything. The expectation of rational thought is, ultimately, to learn all there is to know—an intolerable burden for the finite brain!—and thereby to predict everything accurately. Physicists, unfortunately for that expectation, are discovering more and more that there exists a fundamental uncertainty that makes it impossible to be absolutely sure even of such things as measurements. Scientists no longer expect to be able to predict the future, no matter how complete the information available to them. Nor, they now realize, could any imaginable formula make it possible for

41

some super-being to replicate the universe: Rationalism is simply not an adequate tool for arriving at the final explanation for anything.

The universe, in other words, is no longer seen to be bound by the rules of logic.

LOGIC AND INTUITION

Judging the matter in human terms, the inadequacy of logic is a good thing from several points of view. One is that reasoning, unchecked by calm feeling, leads to pride. Another is that an excess of logic produces what has been termed the Hamlet complex. In other words, "sicklied o'er with the pale cast of thought," it saps the will to act.

Great scientists, despite their insistence on the need for objectivity, cannot but be enthusiastic about their work—in other words, to feel deeply about it. Without enthusiasm, they would never have become great scientists.

Great scientists also depend more on intuition than even they realize. Einstein discovered the Law of Relativity in a flash of intuitive insight; it was only years later that he was able to justify his discovery logically to other scientists. The same is true of all scientific hypotheses: First comes intuition, which conceives them. Only then comes the painstaking process of reasoning it all out persuasively for others.

Edison tested 43,000 filaments before finding the right one for the electric light bulb. His assistants pleaded with him, after 20,000 failures, to give up the attempt. It was his intuitive certainty that such a filament existed that drove him to keep on trying until he succeeded.

Logic itself is a more intuitive process than most people realize. At every stage of the reasoning process one is faced with numerous alternative directions, and with countless others, no doubt, of which one isn't even aware. Without intuition, the sharper the intellect, the greater the uncertainty as to which of all those directions to take. Although one's conclusion may appear as the culmination of a step-by-step process of reasoning, it always involves sudden leaps of understanding—one at the end, especially, which outstrips the carefully logical development. Indeed, without those sudden intuitive leaps the mind would never be satisfied with its conclusions no matter how reasonable they seemed.

MEDITATION AND REASON

Effective meditation, for its part, depends just as much on common sense. If, for example, during meditation you feel "inspired" in a way that defies good judgment, or that contradicts the highest teachings of the ages, you should be warned that something is amiss. Meditative insights, like the hypotheses of science, must be tested in the hard light of objectivity. If they cannot be so verified, they should at least be held suspect.

Objectivity is the criterion in any search for truth, whether it be physics or metaphysics.

I pointed out in Chapter 1 that consciousness could not have come into manifestation had it not already existed before the appearance of creation itself. When people think of pure consciousness, they usually visualize some abstract mental state like "the cosmic ground of being," a favorite among Christian theologians. The state they contemplate, in other words, is one from which feeling is totally absent. There is nothing inspiring, surely, about such abstractions. Without Love, how can we identify that nebulous fog with God? Indeed, how can we think of it at all?

THE IMPORTANCE OF FEELING

If consciousness existed from the beginning, so also, and by the same token, did feeling. And if feeling, then also love, joy, and other *feeling* aspects of consciousness. As reason is a manifestation of the wisdom-aspect of consciousness, so is emotion a manifestation of the feeling-aspect. It is difficult even to imagine consciousness that doesn't include feeling of some kind.

The intuitive feeling of *rightness* that a scientist experiences when he discovers the right answer to a problem is what makes that answer meaningful to him, and through him to others. Were it not for the sheer beauty of logical, but unexpected, deductions in mathematics, it is doubtful whether anyone would feel inspired to become a mathematician. Were it not, indeed, for the feeling aspect of human nature, a case might be made for the claim of materialists that human beings are nothing but sophisticated robots. That KGB torturer mentioned in Chapter 1 was able to tell his victim that she had "no more consciousness than that concrete wall over there" only because he had suppressed all feeling in his own heart.

There is no need to exclude feeling from the search for truth. Nor is it even possible to do so, any more than it is possible to exclude consciousness. To attempt to be unfeeling in one's search is merely, to that extent, to dull one's awareness. Feeling is as intrinsic to awareness as heat is to fire. Both reason and emotion are the filters through which Pure Consciousness enters the physical brain and nervous system. They are not in themselves pure states of consciousness. Pure love and joy are cosmic, not human, realities. They exist far above the emotions—as aspects of Pure Consciousness itself. Human love and happiness, along with every other human emotion, are filtrates of intuitive feeling, just as reason is a filtrate of intuitive wisdom.

Pure love and wisdom are aspects of divine consciousness, and can be perceived only in superconsciousness. Calm feeling is intuition. When that calm feeling is disturbed, as only the ego with its likes and dislikes can disturb it, it becomes emotion. Calm feeling is like a lake without ripples; emotion is like ripples appearing on the surface of the lake, that change the appearance of whatever is reflected there.

To perceive Pure Consciousness, it is not enough to quiet only the mind: The heart's feelings, too, must be stilled. For it is in the heart that feeling is centered; it is there that the feelings must be purified.

Until clarity of feeling is achieved, the meditator will be forever vacillating in purpose, and will never steel himself to take the final plunge into the Infinite. Without devotion, indeed, in the form of deep yearning for the truth, you will not feel the incentive even to *try* to meditate deeply. Wisdom, without devotion, is like knowing that there is a good restaurant next door, and even committing its entire menu to memory, but not being hungry enough to go there and eat.

The feeling quality is what makes it possible to commit oneself to the spiritual search. It is that same feeling quality, directed outward through the emotions, that accounts for our involvement in material delusion.

THE PRINCIPLE OF DUALITY

The universe is founded on the principle of duality. Everything in existence is balanced by its polar opposite. Heat is balanced by cold; light, by darkness; positive, by negative. In mankind, duality is found in the balancing opposites of male and female, joy and sorrow, love and hatred. Wherever one quality exists, its complementary opposite will be found also. They exist together because each is needed to cancel out the other in absolute perfection.

The overall level of an ocean is not altered by the height of the waves at its surface. The higher any wave, the deeper its respective trough. Our essential consciousness, similarly, remains unaffected by our emotional ups and downs. Pleasure and pain, success and failure, fulfillment and disappointment: These are but waves on the surface of calm, intuitive feeling.

The Law of Duality acts as much in our individual lives as in objective Nature. Not only is every joy balanced in the general scheme of things with a sorrow, but that balance occurs in our subjective lives as well. Because our emotions are tied to the post of ego-consciousness, every joy that we experience emotionally must be balanced *in our own emotions* by an equal and opposite sorrow. Every personal success must be balanced by an equally personal failure; every personal fulfillment must be balanced by a corresponding personal disappointment.

The only state in which joy or other positive feelings are not balanced by opposites is that of superconsciousness. There, the waves of emotion subside in calm, intuitive feeling. Joy, love, and peace are realized, then, as absolutes, not as relativities. For they are attributes of Pure Consciousness.

The farther a pendulum swings in one direction, the farther it must swing back in the opposite direction. As an alcoholic binge is succeeded by a hangover, so an emotional "binge" of any kind is inevitably succeeded by its opposite.

People think to increase their happiness or their success by pushing their "energy-pendulum" in the direction they want it to go—toward more possessions, greater fame, more intense pleasure. They wonder why the pendulum seems always to swing back in the opposite direction. Blindness! How could it do otherwise?

Such is the supreme irony of human existence that the sum total of all our striving must always be the same: zero!

How ironic, that everything we strive for so earnestly should add up to nothing. The entire drama of life, with all its pluses and minuses, its ups and downs, its moments of hope and of despair, brings us back again and again to the status quo. Nothing, really, is ever accomplished—nothing outwardly, anyway. Our only gains are inward, in the refinement of our spiritual understanding.

There come times in this ceaseless cycle of hope and disappointment when we feel repelled by the sheer monotony of it all. Finding ourselves no longer attracted by the excitement of a meaningless chase, we long for rest. But only if rest is sought within can lasting peace be really ours. Any rest we find outwardly—in retirement, let us say, to a quiet cottage by the sea—is as temporary as our emotional joys and sorrows. That "peace" ends when we come to experience it as boredom. When this happens, we set out once again on our former quest for excitement.

And so—interminably—it goes on.

The soul, realizing at last that it will never find contentment so long as it seeks peace outwardly, turns within. And there, finally, in meditation, it finds perfect fulfillment.

BEYOND DUALITY

Fulfillment can never be achieved by reaching out for it, but only by stilling the active and reactive feelings in the heart. The ego, in seeking fulfillment outside itself, mistakes reflections for reality. Yet you yourself *are* the joy you seek. In the restlessness of striving for it, you distort that perfect joy to which there is no opposite.

That Self, which is joy, can be found only when the waves of desire, of likes and dislikes, subside in the mind.

Meditation is the process of neutralizing those waves of feeling, by releasing the ego from involvement with them. To achieve this release, simply observe the waves. Don't agitate them further with the winds of personal concern. Gradually, the waves will subside, and the water will come to reflect in its surface the clear moon of superconsciousness.

There are different degrees of involvement with delusion. All of them, in varying degrees, involve the feeling quality. The deeper the ego-involvement, the deeper the delusion.

The first degree is a simple distraction rather than an intense involvement. Nevertheless, it does constitute a serious obstacle to meditation. I'm referring more to impressions on the mind than to reactive emotions in the heart.

The impressions formed by sense-stimuli linger in the mind to influence the direction of our thoughts. For example, I remember picking strawberries for a month on a farm in upstate New York, following my graduation from high school. For the first few weeks, upon closing my eyes at night to go to sleep I would see nothing but strawberries.

Everyone has similar experiences. You watch a movie, for instance, that has no special meaning for you, but the impressions imprinted on your mind linger annoyingly, especially when you try to go to sleep—or, to meditate. These impressions aren't deep, but they are

49

distracting. Feeling is involved primarily in the pleasure or irritation you derive from those impressions.

If there are too many of them, then, certainly, they add up to a serious disturbance to your inner peace. Try to surround yourself with impressions that will uplift the mind. An important result of so doing will be that your meditations will be deeper.

Likes and dislikes form deeper roots in the consciousness. Whereas impressions are like waves, rising and falling without special reference to the ego, likes and dislikes have a greater resemblance to vortices: They draw feeling-energies to a focus in the ego; they define us *to ourselves,* instead of merely distracting our minds. These vortices are the real bonds of our delusion. It is they above all that need to be dissolved.

The strongest vortices are those of karma—actions, and the results we attract to ourselves as a consequence of those actions.*

An illustration may help to clarify these increasingly deep commitments of will power and energy. Impressions represent the lightest commitment, or no real commitment at all. They may be compared to hearing a violinist practicing next door, but paying little attention to what we hear. Thus, even though the memory of his practice sessions may intrude on our dreams at night, or on our meditations, they have no binding effect on the mind.

Likes and dislikes have a binding effect. They arise when we reach the point where we shudder every time

* The Law of Karma demands that every action be balanced by a compensating return of energy. Kindness is met by kindness. Cruelty is met by cruelty. The system of reward and punishment was not invented by behaviorists. It is rooted in the very structure of the

the violinist plays a note off key. In this case, there is personal involvement in the thought "I wish he'd play in tune!" There is even self-definition in the idea "I can't stand music that is out of tune." There is, in this dislike, an element of bondage, for it implies feeling rotated around the thought of the ego. Some karma is involved in this dislike, because karma is simply movement, even of energy.

Of the three—impressions, likes and dislikes, and karma—impressions are the least binding because they are primarily on a level of ideation; they do not yet involve energy. Likes and dislikes involve more energy, causing the mental ripples, both small and large, to rotate around the ego, forming vortices. There is some karma here. If our dislike becomes so seething, however, that we go next door and smash the violin, our flow of energy has reached the level of material action, and is a stronger karma still, one that will have to be worked out on this material plane.

Thus, meditation practiced for Self-realization must be directed toward calming, and thereby neutralizing, the vortices of ego-feeling. First, we must neutralize our likes and dislikes. Gradually also, in time, we must neutralize the specific karmas born of commitment, through action, to our likes and dislikes.

Thus, we come to the classic definition of yoga (divine union), as it appears in a great Indian treatise, *The Yoga Sutras* [*Aphorisms*] *of Patanjali*. The definition reads, "*Yogas chitta vritti nirodha*"—"Yoga is the neutralization of the vortices in the feeling aspect of consciousness."

universe, as the means by which humanity learns, however slowly, in which direction true happiness lies.

51

Our material involvement isn't due only to our mental definition of the world as an apparent reality. (In fact the definition is delusive.) It is our desire for, and our enjoyment or despair of, the world that ensure our bondage to it. Our first task in meditation is to still these likes and dislikes.

To some extent, we accomplish this end by simply watching our likes and dislikes impersonally, while disengaging our egos from personal involvement. The *Bhagavad Gita* makes it clear that we cannot escape the coils of karma by merely not acting. We have to act out our outward karma, but with an attitude of inner non-engagement.

Thus, the impersonality required both in an intellectually honest and a spiritual search for truth entails, not the suppression of feeling, but the refinement of feeling to calm, intuitive awareness.

In calm, intuitive feeling, science and meditation meet.

In watching the mind or the fluctuations of feeling, it is important to do so from the right *place,* mentally. The practice of *vipasana* ("mindfulness") has become popular nowadays, but it has been found in many cases to increase stress instead of decreasing it. Difficulties arise when people do their "watching," not from a place of inner detachment, but in a state of intense mental involvement.

Vipasana is suitable only for those who have already achieved a degree of inner peace. This practice is unsuitable for people who are caught up in the hurry and excitement of busy lives.

While watching your mental process, do so from above, as it were—that is to say, from a higher level of awareness. As much as possible, practice "mindfulness" from a superconscious level. For the conscious mind cannot easily achieve self-understanding. Clear insight comes from superconsciousness.

The following meditation exercise is adapted to that kind of watchfulness which produces inner calmness.

****

MEDITATION EXERCISE

Visualize your heart's feelings as a boundless lake. Strive to see reflected in that lake the full moon in the sky above. Ripples in the lake's surface, and deeper vortices churning below its surface, disturb that reflection. This agitation is due to disturbances in your heart's feelings, past as well as present.

Calm that movement—not by suppressing it, but by seeking at the center of every ripple and vortex the undistorted reflection of the moon above.

You do not have to work to develop divine love. The calmer your lake of feeling, the more clearly and spontaneously will love and devotion appear, reflected, in the heart.

Love is the very essence of reality.

Chapter Four

MEDITATION AND THE PATHS OF YOGA

Whereas there are many religions, there is only one spiritual path. What determines the path is human nature, and—even more definitely—the way the human body is made. Systems of belief have no more to do with determining either human nature or the way the body functions than with determining the movements of the planets. A person may be Christian, Jewish, or follow any other religion, or no religion: The basic realities of human nature, and of the body, remain the same.

The spiritual path serves one purpose, primarily: to uplift human consciousness. The way of upliftment is to deepen people's awareness of their own reality. This reality must be discovered: It cannot be invented. All the religions of the world teach love, service, and harmonious interaction between people—not because the founders of those religions were too timid or sentimental to face the basically predatory nature of human beings. This aggressiveness, loudly proclaimed by many of today's so-called "thinkers," deserves the classic response "Speak for yourself, John." Rather, the founders of the great religions had plumbed human nature to its depths, by facing it first in themselves, and not by reading about it in the theories of others. They were universally acclaimed for their wisdom because they taught what people knew, on deepest levels of consciousness, of themselves.

Truth-teachings through the ages have inspired people to become more kind, loving, humble, and truthful—not because Jesus, Moses, or any other great teacher insisted that this is how *God* wants us to be, but because it is, fundamentally, what resonates with our own nature. It is a universal human experience that people with these qualities have what everyone wants: happiness, and peace of mind. Those other people, on the contrary, who lack these qualities are forever restless and never really happy.

Christians love Jesus Christ for the perfection of his love. It isn't that they hold love in high regard because Jesus loved. Certain principles are timeless and universal. Religious dogmas, if they are valid, are so because they formulate those timeless principles clearly and well.

Regardless of our religious beliefs, spiritual upliftment is determined also by the way our bodies are made. The spine, brain, and nervous system are universal facts, not only of human beings, but of all vertebrate life. They play a vital role in the ability of human beings, especially, to perceive reality.

The purpose of religion is universally the same: the upliftment of human consciousness. Upliftment is not a specifically Christian or Jewish or any other sort of phenomenon, even as modern science is not a specifically Western phenomenon. Science is science. Upliftment is upliftment.

The goal of meditation is to achieve superconsciousness. Meditation practices, as many define them, can include certain forms of worship for which superconsciousness is an indirect goal, while their immediate aim is to commemorate some historical event, or to reflect on some scriptural teaching. Meditation as I discuss it in this book is that kind of concentration which is focused directly on the attainment of superconsciousness.

THE ART AND SCIENCE OF YOGA

Of all spiritual practices, the oldest and most complete is the science and art of yoga. The yoga tradition contains many systems, all of them with superconsciousness as their final goal.

Yoga means, simply, "union." Implied, of course, is the concept of divine union. External paths to this goal are, like tributary streams, the paths of action (*karma yoga*), of devotion (*bhakti yoga*), and of discrimination (*gyana yoga,* or *jnana* as it is sometimes transliterated). The internal path of meditation (*raja yoga*) is the river into which these tributaries flow.

The usage of Sanskrit terms has become widespread in the West. I'll try to limit my use of them for the sake of the average Western reader. In fairness to that same reader, however, it is necessary to use Sanskrit terms when the English translation falls short of conveying their full meaning. To translate *karma yoga*, for instance, literally as "the path of action" is misleading, for it doesn't make clear what kind of action is implied.

Karma yoga signifies freeing oneself from one's karmic bonds, a suggestion that is lost by substituting the word "action" for *karma*. *Bhakti yoga*, similarly, implies an intimacy of love that is lacking in what many people call the "path of devotion," for devotion is associated in many people's minds with formal rituals and ceremonial practices. And *gyana yoga* signifies the practice of discriminating in such a way as to lead to the unfoldment of wisdom. The way of *gyana yoga*, then, involves intuitive perception, not merely intellectual analysis as suggested by the translation, "the path of discrimination."

Nor, rightly speaking, are any of these even paths, though people generally refer to them as such. A path is a specific route, one that therefore excludes other routes. But the "paths" of yoga cannot be so separated one from another. They are intended for three basic types of human beings, yet no human being belongs exclusively to one type or another.

Karma yoga is for active types. *Karma yoga* as a teaching, however, also provides guidelines for everyone. For no one can live without performing action of some sort. The *Bhagavad Gita* declares that even to do nothing is a kind of action. The mind is not stilled thereby, nor are countless involuntary functions of the body suspended.

Bhakti yoga is for those who live more by emotional feeling. The teachings, however, make clear the need for every human being to refine and uplift his feelings, that they flow upward to God.

Gyana yoga is for those who go primarily by intellect, but it also teaches everyone how to direct his native intelligence toward the highest truth in any situation.

No one's temperament is limited to only one of these aspects. None of us, in other words, is *only* active, or guided *only* by his emotions or intellect. No one can avoid depending on each of these three aspects of human nature at various times in his life.

None of the three yogas, moreover, can be practiced perfectly on its own. Devotion needs discrimination, lest it become merely emotional. Discrimination needs devotion, lest it sink into inaction. Action requires both devotion and discrimination, or it may take the mind into mere restlessness. And both devotion and discrimination require action to make them practical, for they may wander off in mere sentiment or in endless theorizing.

The three yogas, in other words, are intended to be seen as complementary to one another, as means of developing the complete human being.

Karma Yoga

The term *karma yoga* means "to behave in such a way as to direct our energies Godward." The classic teaching regarding *karma yoga* is found in the *Bhagavad Gita:* "*nishkam karma*" ("action without desire for the fruits of action"). People who say "I am practicing *karma yoga*" to excuse the fact that they don't meditate, when in fact they may be busily engaged in amassing a fortune, are practicing *karma* all right, but not *karma yoga*.

Karma yoga intends to cut the bonds of ego involvement by acting out, in the right way, impulses that were set into motion in the wrong way in the past. Spiritually harmful impulses can be redirected into constructive tendencies. Avarice, for example, can be overcome by practicing generosity. The wish to harm others can be purified by serving them selflessly.

Try, when practicing *karma yoga,* to see God, rather than your little ego, as the Doer. It is easier to transform good than bad karma into spiritual awareness—easier, for example, for a generous person than for a miser to develop an expansive consciousness—but the more one realizes that self-fulfillment is the equivalent of self-expansion, the more clearly one feels motivated to expand one's sense of self to infinity.

Perfection in *karma yoga* leads to transmuting the impulse to act at all from ego-consciousness. The consequence of this transmutation is superconsciousness, and perfect inner stillness.

Bhakti Yoga

The practice of *bhakti yoga* is intended to awaken the emotions, but after awaking them to calm and focus them, not to agitate them.

As floating debris is drawn into the wake of a ship, so the desire for worldly satisfaction is drawn into the "wake" of intense devotional yearning for God.

Again, just as our daily responsibilities pale into insignificance before some overwhelming tragedy—the death, for example, of someone dear to us—so our lesser attachments loosen their grip on our minds when we are overwhelmed by intense pangs of separation from God.

Chanting to God, calling to Him with ever increasing zeal, stirring up devotional yearning in the heart—all of these are examples of *bhakti yoga.*

But if the heart's feelings, once awakened, are not withdrawn and directed upward in calm meditation, they fuel the emotions, merely, which agitate the heart's feelings and carry them outward, not upward to our source in God.

Saints who have achieved perfection in *bhakti yoga* have become rapt in ecstasy, where the only possible expression of their love was an expansion of inner silence.

As Paramhansa Yogananda wrote once, "Oh, how maddening! I can pray no more with words, but only with wistful yearning."

Bhakti (devotion) is fulfilled not by loud chanting, but in the attainment of inner silence, in super-consciousness.

GYANA YOGA

Gyana yoga, finally, requires that the questions be asked constantly in the mind, What? Why? Who? Where? "What is the true goal of life? Why is it the true goal? Who am I that seek that true goal? Where shall I find that goal?"

At first, as in the other tributaries, or bypaths, of yoga, the discrimination is directed outward: "What makes people behave as they do? Is their motivation what they think it is? What are their deeper motivations? *Why* are they motivated?"

Careful observation reveals a common purpose that runs threadlike through the tapestry of everything that people do: the coarse thread of selfish motive.

The discriminating yogi asks, "Is this motive good? Is it bad? What makes it either good or bad?" In time, he comes to realize that ego-motive that is self-contractive rather than self-expansive is obstructive to happiness. Only self-expansion gives the broad fulfillment that all human beings seek.

Again, the *gyana yogi,* in the contemplation of life, realizes that the objective world is not much different from the dream world we enter in sleep. "Is not human life, then," he asks himself, "merely another kind of dream? What, in the last analysis, is reality?"

He observes suffering, old age, and death, as the Buddha did, and asks himself, "Is this the whole story of existence? Is there no state of being from which these universal miseries are forever absent?" Discrimination leads him to this conclusion: "There *must* be such a state! Otherwise, why have I this conviction in my soul that nothing else is real? Perfection must be a potential of life if only because, were it not so, the desire for it could not have arisen in my mind."

Finally, there arises the fundamental question of the *gyana yogi:* "Who am I?" This question demands an increasingly inward focus. For who is it that is asking the question? The intellect can provide no answer. The mind thus reaches a state of inner stillness.

Neti, neti is the practice of the *gyana yogi:* "Not this, not that." Discrimination, practiced unceasingly, reveals nothing to be substantial—no thing, no fulfillment, no grief—nothing.

What is left, then? Nothing! The practice of *neti, neti* leads the mind to the "nothingness" of perfect silence: superconsciousness.

RAJA YOGA

In the three "tributaries," as I have called them, of yoga, perfection is attained in superconscious stillness. Thus, the path of meditation is called *raja yoga,* the kingly yoga. *Raja yoga* is the river into which flow the tributary streams of *karma, bhakti,* and *gyana yoga*s. These three tributaries are based on the basic qualities of human nature, whereas *raja yoga* transcends human nature in its emphasis on eternal qualities of the soul. Since superconscious meditation is the culmination of all the other yogas, anyone seeking the highest spiritual attainment should include in his spiritual search the daily practice of meditation.

****

MEDITATION PRACTICE

Meditate on the heart. Think of it as a lotus, its petals, like rays of energy, turned upward toward the brain.

Visualize each petal as a specific aspect of your feelings: love, aspiration, enthusiasm, longing, tenderness, fiery devotion, self-dedication, renunciation of lesser goals in life. Direct all of these aspects upward, toward superconsciousness.

Visualize, now, the mud out of which the lotus grows, as it lifts itself high into the air to absorb the sunlight. The lotus looks upward, away from the mud of its origins. Yet it cannot deny those origins, lest it die. Think of it as sustained by them—turned away not in contempt, but gratefully, in its aspiration toward higher realities.

Do not mentally reject what you've been in the past. See God's presence there also, in the mud of your human origins. See God rising through long, arduous effort to reclaim Himself in the Great Self; God in the sunlight; God as the eternally shining, ever-blissful Sun.

Chapter Five

THE BASIC ATTITUDES
OF YOGA

Spiritual progress should be natural, not forced—like a growing tree, not like the frenetic struggle of minor actors to achieve fame.

Think how many things you do in the hope of resting *after* you've finished them. "Let me buy that racy sports car," you think, "or that handsome station wagon for the whole family. *Then* I'll be able to relax and really enjoy life."

Or you may think, "Once I get that new house, with the shaded porch and the large master bedroom; that sunny dining room so we won't have to eat any longer in the kitchen with the cucumbers; that sunken living room—ah, *then* I'll find peace and be able to enjoy life at last!"

Thus you acquire the habit of looking for more and more things, more and more ways of resting better and enjoying life more fully *after* the acquisition or *after* the accomplishment. The irony is that in the very seeking you lose the capacity to rest at all. Thus you never really get to enjoy life. Experiencing more and more stress in the seeking, you lose the ability to relax even after you've "arrived."

An important rule in life is: Don't be impatient. This rule is doubly important for meditation, for whereas the general stricture against impatience gives hope of finding inner peace in meditation, that hope is demolished if one applies to meditation itself attitudes that we've developed in the "rat race." To find God, it is better to be a long-distance runner than a sprinter. Today's meditative efforts will have to be renewed tomorrow, and again the day after tomorrow, and the day after that, and so on for as long as it takes to achieve the consciousness of the Eternal Now.

Paramhansa Yogananda was asked once, "Does the spiritual path have any end?" "No end," he replied. "You go on until you achieve endlessness."

Don't let your approach to meditation be so achievement-oriented that you end up mentally tense. Yogananda, noting my own tendency toward impatience, once said to me, "The principle of *karma yoga* applies to meditative action also. Meditate to please God. Don't meditate with desire for the fruits of your meditations. It is best, in the beginning, to emphasize relaxation."

Of course what he meant was, Don't desire fruits that accrue to your ego. For it is the ego, not the soul, that experiences impatience. Patience is the fastest path to God, because it develops soul-consciousness.

The more you seek rest as the consequence of doing, rather than in the process of doing, the more restless you will become. Peace isn't waiting for you over the next hill. Nor is it something you construct, like a building. It must be a part of the creative process itself.

Learn to be restful, even in the midst of activity, and you will be able to relax better when you sit to meditate. As Paramhansa Yogananda put it, "Be calmly active, and actively calm."

THE NEED TO CLARIFY THE SUBCONSCIOUS

The greatest obstacle to spiritual progress is that vast terrain of the mind which, to a great extent, conditions our understanding of life without our being aware of the conditioning process. I am referring to the subconscious mind.

For it isn't only our conscious decisions that determine our outlook on life and our accomplishments. In the subconscious lie vast farmlands in need of plowing and cultivation—or, less figuratively, in need of purification and refinement, lest crosscurrents of unnoticed desires and attachments obstruct our every worthwhile undertaking.

The subconscious cannot be bullied. It must be coaxed, and its energies carefully redirected. At the end of the chapter I'll suggest a method for accomplishing this end.

It is a misnomer, in discussing the subconscious, to label it (as many do) the "unconscious." There is nothing unconscious about it. Indeed, there is nothing unconscious about anything. Not even the rocks are totally unconscious. There is only that aspect of consciousness of which we are not dynamically aware, in the conscious mind. In a country, this aspect would rep-resent that segment of society which aristocrats used snobbishly to write off as the "great unwashed." It is the unprocessed residue of thoughts, actions, and memories that are ever present, but more or less unnoticed. They greatly influence the conscious mind, which doesn't often realize how ungoverned by free will its decisions really are.

Thoughts and actions, frequently repeated, form habit patterns in the subconscious mind. Habits can be positive as well as negative. Positively, they free the con-scious mind to concentrate on other things.

For example, because we've developed the subcon-scious habit of tying our shoelaces a certain way, we can perform that act automatically, while chatting effort-lessly and planning with others the program for the day. If we had to tie our shoelaces with all the care and delib-eration of a child learning the job for the first time, all our concentration would have to be focused on that simple act.

Habit is an important labor-saving device of the mind. Without it, we'd be greatly limited in our freedom to accomplish anything.

Habit is also, however, an unthinking and undiscrim-inating servant. If we repeat a wrong action often enough, our subconscious will direct us to keep on repeating it, even without our conscious awareness of its power to influence us.

There are several ways to gain the upper hand over this domestic staff, our subconscious thoughts and habits.

One way is to make sure we give them only good commands, by performing good actions and entertaining uplifting thoughts.

Another way is to starve the subconscious of bad impulses by refusing to feed it any more bad thoughts and actions.

Still another way is to channel self-damaging impulses more wholesomely, in an opposite direction. For example, if we have an impulse toward avarice, we can acquire things as we normally feel impelled to do, but then give them away to others.

If our wrong habits are too strong to resist, we can at least resist them mentally, thereby withholding energy from them. While starving them in this way, we should give strong energy to creating or strengthening good habits.

The best way to change the subconscious is from above—that is, from the level of superconsciousness. For the conscious mind is an unreliable soldier in this War of Soul-Independence. Just when you most need it, you find it has gone AWOL—"absent without leave"— and is perhaps soaking it up in some local bar. Conscious decisions are tainted by influences of which the conscious mind is not even aware. We say we are free to do what we like, but what makes us like to do what we do? It isn't that attractiveness is inherent in those things. Likes and dislikes are subjective. They rise to the conscious level from the subconscious, and keep us bound to the world's delusions whether we consciously agree or not. Merely to recognize a fault intellectually, or to recognize a rationalization as being subconsciously inspired, is no guarantee of readiness on our part to be rid of it.

Essential to effective meditation is a restful heart. Merely to affirm restfulness, however, is like affirming fullness in a milk pail riddled with holes. We must take practical steps to *achieve* restfulness. The holes in the pail must first be plugged. If they are not, you may keep on milking the cow, but your best efforts will at best have only temporary benefits.

THE FIRST TWO STAGES: THE TEN "COMMANDMENTS" OF YOGA

The yoga teachings list ten attitudes for meditators. Five of them are proscriptive; the other five, prescriptive: the "don'ts" and the "do's" of the spiritual path. The importance of these attitudes is that they prevent our energy from "leaking" out. This they accomplish first by plugging the holes in the pail, and next by helping us to accumulate the "milk" of inner peace.

The fact that these attitudes number ten invites comparison with the Ten Commandments of Moses. There is, however, a difference. For the *yamas* and *niyamas* are not commandments so much as recommendations. Their emphasis is not on what you will suffer if you break them, but on what your benefits will be from following them. They are *directions* of development. One can continue to perfect them indefinitely, until one attains spiritual perfection.

THE FIRST *YAMA: AHIMSA*

The "don'ts" are listed first. The holes must be plugged before the pail can be filled. These five attitudes are grouped under the heading of *yama* (control). It may seem strange to see these principles stated negatively. The reason for this is that they stand revealed as virtues when their opposite, negative qualities are removed. Each rule of *yama* serves the purpose, similarly, of permitting innate virtues to flower. Figuratively speaking, every *yama* removes the dirt covering the true gold of our being. What is left, once a negative tendency has been removed, is a soul-reality.

The first rule of *yama* was popularized by Mahatma Gandhi. It is *ahimsa* (non-violence). The reason for this negative emphasis (it could have been translated as "benevolence") is that once a person succeeds in banishing from his heart the impulse to strike out at others, or to hurt them in any way (including seeking personal benefit at their expense), benevolence stands self-revealed as a natural quality of the heart.

The desire to hurt another living being in any way—or even to harm our environment, which too, in varying degrees, is alive and conscious—alienates us from our soul-reality, and affirms the delusion of ego.

Anything that separates us in consciousness from the vastness of all life amounts to a denial of that oneness which we should be seeking in meditation.

The important thing in all the attitudes of *yama* and *niyama* is not so much what we do outwardly, as our *inner* attitudes of the heart. It is not possible to live harmlessly, for example, in this world of relativities.

Some harm is done, inevitably, by merely living. With every inhalation, hosts of germs are killed. Every outing in the car inadvertently causes the death of numerous insects. We walk out of doors and can hardly avoid stepping on a few ants. Nature herself decrees the survival of life by the death of other life. Even the vegetables we eat are life forms. It is a tiger's nature to kill: Can its method of survival, then, be considered sinful? Murder is a sin for human beings for the primary reason that it degrades us, at our level of evolution, to kill other human beings. Murder is the opposite of life-affirming. It is an affirmation of death.* Otherwise, it must be said that, from a broad perspective, death comes to all of us eventually. It cannot be, then, in itself, an evil.

There are situations, the *Bhagavad Gita* declares, in which a lesser harm must be inflicted to forestall a greater harm, and when to shrink from such a duty is itself an act of violence. Thus, at times it is necessary to fight—for example, in a defensive war. Again, according to karmic law, more highly evolved species should be protected from less evolved species, even if the protection involves killing. In the case of righteous warfare, the protection required is not that of a higher from a lower species, but that of a higher *purpose* from lower motives—safety of the innocent, for instance, from the will of an aggressor to destroy.

In every case, the essential rule of *ahimsa,* and that which removes it from relativity's uncertainties, is that the spiritual seeker maintain at all times a non-violent *attitude.*

---

*I have read not a few statements to the effect that "hit men" and other professional killers have what are described as "dead" eyes.

By wishing harm to no living creature, even if it becomes necessary to kill it, we find welling up within ourselves a consciousness of relaxed acceptance of others and of life, no matter how we ourselves are treated. Thus, in the conscious benevolence that arises with acceptance, we find others responding to us accordingly. When we perfect the quality of non-violence, hostility ceases in our presence.

For the purposes of meditation, non-violence has a further purpose. The wish to inflict harm creates in ourselves an inner tension, which conflicts with the peacefulness we seek to develop in meditation.

THE SECOND *YAMA*: TRUTHFULNESS

Another principle of the "don'ts" is "avoidance of untruthfulness." Why, again, is this teaching stated negatively? Wouldn't it be simpler to say "Be truthful"? The explanation is that our natural tendency *is* to be truthful, once we've overcome the desire to distort the truth.

There is in this quality, also, a subtle as well as a gross application. For fact and truth are not always synonymous. A statement may be factual without bearing any relationship to higher truths. A person in the hospital, for example, may look quite as ill as he feels, but if you tell him, "You look terrible!" your statement might actually worsen his condition. If, on the other hand, visualizing him in good health, you declare with deep conviction, "You look great!" your words may invigorate or even heal him.

Here is a guideline to practicing the avoidance of untruthfulness. Bear in mind that the truth is always beneficial, but that a statement of fact may be either beneficial or harmful. If there is a chance that a statement will do harm, it must not be considered a truth in the highest sense. If you cannot speak sincerely without the risk of inflicting harm, the best alternative is to remain silent. (That may be one reason why certain ascetics in India practice perpetual *mauna* [silence]!)

Avoidance of untruthfulness is an important practice also for meditation. For the mind, influenced by tendencies that well up from the subconscious, is easily inclined toward self-deception. Hallucinations are an obstacle that people encounter in meditation; they are not visual, only, but may take other delusive forms—for example, "intuitive" guidance. Because they come from the subconscious, their effect is to draw the mind downward, away from superconsciousness.

There is a certain attractiveness in the passively pleasant world of the subconscious. It is easy to become caught in it, instead of rising on wing-beats of will power into the lofty regions of ecstasy. The mystical literature of all religions contains warnings against subconscious self-deception.

How is one to know when one is hallucinating? By testing the experience in the "cold light of day." For one thing, true superconscious experiences are accompanied by intense inner awareness. They also produce beneficial and lasting results. Since an emotion, too, may be intense, it is important to add that the intensity accompanying superconscious experiences will also be calm.

There is nothing dull or vague about superconscious experiences. If a light is seen in superconsciousness, it will be a clear light, not smoky or indistinct. Any inspiration felt produces mental clarity, not vagueness or confusion. In matters where clarity was lacking previously, the experience produces clear insight and understanding. Often, the clarity will receive external substantiation.

Perfection in the avoidance of untruthfulness develops mental power to such an extent that one's mere word becomes binding on objective events. One has merely to declare a thing so for it actually to become so.

At this point, it becomes extremely important that our every statement be positive and kindly, at least in intent. (There is no way of determining other people's reactions.) For negative or unkind thoughts have the power to do harm.

THE THIRD *YAMA*: NON-AVARICE

Another *yama* is "non-avarice."* "Avarice" is not really the *mot juste,* implying as it does a desire for worldly gain (money, usually, or something of monetary value). The *yama* of non-avarice implies something much deeper.

---

*This word is often, but superficially, translated as "non-stealing." To tell a thief that he should give up thieving is fair enough, but to make it one of ten basic "commandments" for people on the spiritual path that they give up stealing seems to me ludicrous. Rare indeed must that meditator be for whom stealing constitutes a serious problem!

What the spiritual seeker must renounce is the desire for anything that he does not acquire by merit. The implication is that if he does merit it, he needn't fear that he won't attract it. Even if he must work hard to attract it, he should remain relaxed as to the outcome, leaving the results wholly in God's hands. "What comes of itself, let it come" is his motto. This is a prescription for peace of mind even during intense activity.

Things are not often achieved effortlessly. The attitude of non-avarice, then, is not to stop striving, but even in the process of striving to renounce attachment to the results.

The secret of inner peace is desirelessness. In meditation, desire for anything external to oneself takes the mind out of the true Self, within. Any desire that pulls the mind outward works against success in meditation.

While meditating, then, tell yourself that you need nothing: You are complete in yourself. You are at perfect peace within. Say to yourself, "I own nothing: I am free! I own no one: I am free! In myself I am ever perfect, ever free!"

The quality of non-avarice, developed to perfection, generates a subtle magnetism that enables a person to attract things to himself effortlessly. He is never anxious, then, that his needs, whatever they may be, won't be supplied. They *will* be, infallibly.

THE FOURTH *YAMA*: NON-ACCEPTANCE

A natural corollary to the *yama* of "non-avarice" is "non-acceptance." Some authorities have understood this word (*aparigraha*) to mean the non-acceptance of gifts, the idea being that to accept them might incur a karmic debt. This explanation is inadequate, however, as becomes clear from an examination of the power said to develop with the perfection of this principle. Non-acceptance, when brought to perfection, bestows the power to remember one's past incarnations.

To remember our past lives, we must withdraw our consciousness and energy from the body and enter a state of superconsciousness. It is only when the soul is not identified with its present body that it remembers its previous identities.

"Non-acceptance," then, pairs naturally with "non-avarice." Non-avarice signifies non-attachment to what is not our own; non-acceptance signifies non-attachment to what we would normally consider to be our own. The point is that nothing, truly, belongs to us. Everything—our bodies, our actions, our very thoughts—is the Lord's.

If, in meditation, you give yourself so completely to God that you realize the truth that all is His, you will attain results quickly.

This fourth attitude, as I've listed it here, is listed fifth by Patanjali, the authority in this field. I've changed his placement only to clarify the natural contrast between non-avarice and non-acceptance. There has been considerable confusion on these two points, partly for the very reason that they are separated in their traditional listing. Evidently, Patanjali chose to put non-acceptance last for another reason: It leads naturally into the next set of attitudes, the *niyamas*.

THE FIFTH YAMA: BRAHMACHARYA

The last *yama,* though placed fourth in Patanjali's *Aphorisms,* is *brahmacharya*—self-control, or, more literally, "flowing with Brahma (the Supreme Spirit)." Usually, this teaching is applied to the practice of sexual abstinence. It has also, however, a broader application. For *brahmacharya* means control of every natural appetite, of which sexual desire is the strongest but not the only one.

The ideal behind this teaching is to live identified with the Spirit, realizing ourselves as the soul living through the body, and no longer as the ego centered in body-consciousness. We should live in such a way as to master our appetites, and not allow ourselves to be mastered by them.

The recommendation here is not extreme abstinence, although complete sexual abstinence is at least a possibility. The important thing is to achieve self-control, first by moderation, directing our efforts only gradually toward perfect self-control.

To accomplish self-control, the seeker is taught even in the midst of enjoyment to direct that sense of enjoyment upward to the brain. He should try to feel that sensory pleasure is feeding his inner joy at its source in the Self.

There is an amusing story about George Bernard Shaw, the playwright, who inadvertently illustrated this principle. He was sitting alone on the outskirts of a party when the hostess came over and asked him, "Are you enjoying yourself?" He replied, "That's all I am enjoying!"

We should seek, in a similar spirit, to discern behind every outer experience the joy of our own being.

In meditation, especially, seek the flow of pure joy in the spine. That is the true river of baptism, outwardly symbolized in many religions as a river, but actually experienced as a mighty current in the deep spine. It is here alone that the seeker's consciousness is purified.

Many saints in various religions have made light of the human need to replace inner truths with outer symbols. A saint in India remarked, smiling, "Oh, it's no doubt true that your sins leave you when you bathe in the holy river Ganges. But they sit in the trees along the bank, and the moment you come out of the water they jump on you all over again!" Bathe, then, in the peace of meditation, and especially in the river of the spine. That is where you will experience true, spiritual baptism.

The power that comes through perfect control of all our natural appetites is an accession of boundless energy. For our energy and, indeed, all that we can express of creativity and enthusiasm flow the more strongly, the more we can tap the wellsprings of life within ourselves.

THE NIYAMAS

The *niyamas*, or "do's," of the path of meditation number five also, as I said earlier. They are cleanliness, contentment, austerity, introspection (self-study, or self-awareness), and devotion to the Supreme Lord.

Again, these qualities must be understood subtly. "Cleanliness," for example, applies to purity of the heart far more than to bodily cleanliness, though of course it includes the latter. "Contentment" is not smugness, but an attitude that one should hold courageously in the face of the greatest vicissitudes. "Austerity" is not the performance of outward penances, but an attitude of dis-involvement with outwardness. Introspection (self-study, or self-awareness) would seem to be directed more obviously inward, but it implies much more than self-analysis. For self-analysis keeps the mind tied to the ego, whereas what is meant, primarily, is to hold the mind up for guidance by the silent whispers of intuition. Devotion to the Supreme Lord, finally, is a reference to devotion that is directed inward, not scattered outwardly in religious ceremonies and rituals.

Interestingly, there is a complementary relationship between the five *niyama*s and their opposite *yama*s. Contentment, for example, is complemented by non-avarice. Introspection (self-study) has a natural correlation to non-acceptance. Austerity ties in with *brahmacharya;* cleanliness, with *ahimsa;* and devotion to the Supreme Lord with the avoidance of untruthfulness.

The positive aspect of non-avarice, and the way to perfect oneself in this quality, is to live with an attitude of contentment regardless of any circumstance.

Non-acceptance, which means not accepting the thought that we own anything, has as its positive aspect the contemplation of being, not of non-being—of what we are, not of what we are not. *Swadhyaya* is the Sanskrit name for this *niyama*. Since *dhyaya* means "study," authorities often translate it to mean "study of the scriptures." *Swa*, however, refers to *self*. "Self-study," then, is a more approximate translation of the word. And since all the *yama-niyama*s refer more to mental qualities than to outer practices, *swadhyaya* has a deeper meaning than intellectual self-analysis. It is a reference, rather, to ever deeper self-awareness—a process that transcends mental introspection and requires us to see ourselves and everything around us in relation to the higher, divine Self. "Dwell always," it tells us, "in the consciousness of the Self within."

With the dawning of this consciousness, we become aware of the Lord as our true Self.

AUSTERITY, CLEANLINESS, DEVOTION

Austerity is the natural corollary to *brahmacharya* (self-control), for it means an attitude of taking energy that was formerly directed outwardly, and rechanneling it with ever increasing fervor into the spiritual search.

"Cleanliness" pairs naturally with *ahimsa* (non-violence). For only by renouncing the desire to do violence in any way to others do we develop that sweet innocence which is the surest sign of a heart inwardly pure and at peace. From cleanliness arises a disinterest in one's own body, and a loss of the need for contact with others. The need for human contact arises from a consciousness of separateness from others. Mental acceptance of separateness is, in its own way, an act of violence, for it offends against the realization of life's underlying unity. With perfection in non-violence we achieve that absolute inner purity which is recommended by the *niyama* of cleanliness.

"Devotion to the Supreme Lord," finally, pairs with "avoidance of untruthfulness." For perfect truthfulness entails far more than the truthfulness of George Washington's famous confession, "Father, it was I who cut down the cherry tree." Perfect truthfulness means facing unconditionally that there is only one reality in existence: God. Outside of Him (or Her), we have no existence. To give up the temptation to put off that moment when we must face the ultimate truth about ourselves— this fundamental and utter self-honesty permits of only one conclusion, summed up in the final *niyama:* "Devotion to the Supreme Lord."

CONCLUSION

The *yama-niyama*s are essential for anyone who would sail smoothly on the seas of superconsciousness. For there is no path to God other than recognition of these fundamental verities of our own nature.

Although the qualities described here are listed by the ancient sage Patanjali as the first two stages on the spiritual path, it is not a question of having to perfect them *first,* before proceeding on to the higher stages. Perfection in any aspect of the path requires perfection in all of them. What concerns us here is the perfection, not of deeds—an impossible feat in this relative universe—but of consciousness. Such perfection can be attained only in superconscious union with the Divine.

Be restful in your heart, therefore, even as you work to perfect yourself in right spiritual attitudes. Only by inner restfulness during outer activity will you achieve that supreme restfulness which lies beyond all activity.

****

Meditation Practice

Wisdom descends from superconsciousness. It is from that level that our personalities truly become transformed, our faults eradicated, and our virtues brought to perfection.

Calm your mind in meditation. Center your gaze and attention in the frontal lobe of the brain, at the point between the eyebrows—the seat of superconsciousness in the body.

From that high center, keep your mind focused on the thought that your will power is dynamic, free, and forever joyful. Now, let your mind sink downward into the lower part of the brain—the seat of subconsciousness. Offer up, for purification by the inner light, the tangle of subconscious desires and frustrations. Tell yourself repeatedly, with deep, calm concentration: "I am joyful! I am free! In myself, I am forever free!"

PART II

THE PROCESS

Chapter Six

MEDITATION IS LISTENING

The right attitudes constitute only the beginning of the spiritual journey, though to perfect oneself in them requires the effort of a lifetime, and encompasses the entire spiritual journey. Not only is right attitude necessary for achieving perfection in meditation: It also can be perfected only in meditation.

What, then, is meditation? Here is a good definition: *Meditation is listening*. It is listening not only with the ear, but with the soul—not only to sound, but to the silent language of inspiration. Each of the *yama-niyamas* might be described as a practice for perfection in the art of listening.

Take the first *yama*. Non-violence is listening to the inner silence—listening so sensitively that you perceive clearly the violence you do to your inner peace by inflicting harm on anyone, even in thought.

"Avoidance of untruthfulness" is "listening" to whatever *is*—in this case, learning to accept and to be completely comfortable with what can't be avoided. It means not judging. It means striving to hear, behind the inner silence, the soul's reassurance that all is well and as it should be.

"Non-avarice" means dwelling in the awareness of soul-freedom, the companion of meditative peace. It means "listening" to the silence behind the hubbub of worldly desires in the mind.

"Non-acceptance" is listening to the divine sounds within. (These will be described later.) It means knowing completely that these sounds represent your only reality. To accept anything as belonging to you, even your talents and personality traits, can only obstruct deeper Self-knowing.

Brahmacharya, or control of the natural appetites, is "listening" to your truer, soul-aspirations.

"Cleanliness" is listening to the all-purifying "music of the spheres," heard in deep meditation, as opposed to the peace-besmirching influences of the world.

"Contentment" is listening in another sense: not to the siren-songs of desire, but to the anthem-like harmonies of the soul, enjoyable beyond any imaginable worldly fulfillment.

"Austerity" is listening to the voice of inner wisdom, however stern it may sound at first—to words or inspirations from within that gently but firmly draw us to become dis-involved from activity that pertains to anything but the Self. The very powers that result from perfection in *tapasya* (austerity) are perceived, in deep meditation, as merely temptations of the mind, their real aim being to involve us once again in delusion.

"Self-study" (*swadhyaya*) is, figuratively speaking, "listening" to the melodies of pure motivation, and learning to distinguish between them and the harsh caws of ego-motivation.

"Devotion to the Supreme Lord," finally, is listening intently to the inner "Word," which the Bible tells us was "in the beginning," was "with God," and "was" God. The "Word" is not, as many Christians believe, the Bible itself; nor is it any other scripture. It is *AUM*—the divine sound out of which the universe was manifested.

It is too early at this point to discuss in depth such esoteric experiences as the inner sounds. The important thing, here, is to understand with this mere hint of their existence that meditation is not so much a process of stilling the mind as of perceiving realities that exist beyond the mind. There is an inner world that can be perceived only when the attention has been turned away from material involvement and redirected toward the divine source within.

To repeat, "listening" itself, as I use the word here, entails much more than listening with the ears. It means, among other things, the stillness of expectation, and complete mental absorption in whatever inspirations come. It means *receiving,* as opposed to generating uplifting thoughts with the mind. It includes all of these, while providing to each of them a deeper dimension.

For in fact there is, literally, an inner music which, when heard, removes the mind from all worldly concerns, and banishes the delusion of any existence outside the Self.

Thus, "listening" as applied to the attitudes of *yama-niyama,* as well as to the yoga science in general, clarifies a misconception people frequently have who imagine that yoga teaches self-effort, but scorns the need for divine grace. As Paramhansa Yogananda put it in *Autobiography of a Yogi,* "A truth cannot be created, but only perceived."

Divine grace is forever impersonal. It is not, like the human will, dependent on personal choices or inclinations. It has no favorites. Like the sunlight, it shines impartially everywhere. What keeps the sunlight from arriving equally everywhere is the presence of obstructions: clouds, buildings, the curtains covering a window. What keeps grace from reaching us is obstructions in our consciousness.

We may not be able to do much about obstructions to grace that, like clouds and buildings, are put there by Nature or by other people—illness, for example, or negative thought forms—but we *can* draw back the curtains that cover the windows of our own minds. These obstructions are our mental restlessness and worldly desires.*

This, then, is the benefit of yoga practice: It draws back our mental curtains; it helps us to *listen* more intently to the divine call within. It is—to use another illustration—like turning the chalice of thought and feeling right-side up, that the wine of grace may fill it. If, instead, the chalice is turned upside down, grace, which (unlike the sunlight) is superconscious, will simply be withheld. Why should it spill uselessly to the floor?

---

*Paramhansa Yogananda, during an all-day Christmas meditation, had a vision of God as the Divine Mother. After some time he cried, "Don't go! You say the material desires of these people are driving you away? Oh, come back! Please don't go!"

THE THIRD STAGE: *ASANA*—RIGHT POSTURE

The third stage of meditation, after the *yama*s and *niyama*s, is to prepare the mind for meditative listening.

Even in normal concentration, physical stillness is necessary. When a person shoots a rifle, he must hold his hands and his body still. If a shot is particularly difficult, he must even hold his breath.

A photographer, when "shooting" a photograph at a slow exposure, must hold himself—his hands, his body, even his breath—completely still.

Similarly, whenever we need to listen carefully, especially if the person we're listening to is speaking very softly or at a distance, we naturally hold our bodies very still, and breathe as little and as quietly as possible.

For meditation, the first requirement is to keep the body motionless—even, as much as possible, to still the breath. How to accomplish this stillness of the breath? I'll discuss this point later. The question now before us is the first one: how to still the body.

Keep it relaxed. To quiet the body forcibly is to focus the mind on it, instead of on superconsciousness. What we must do is transcend body-consciousness, that our listening become a process of total absorption.

The next requirement for right posture—the only other requirement, in fact—is to keep the spine straight and erect. This position may seem counterproductive for relaxation, but the relaxation required in meditation is a relaxation *upward,* toward superconsciousness, not *downward,* toward subconsciousness.

It is natural, for one who wants to relax physically, to lie flat, surrendering to the force of gravity. There is, however, another kind of "gravity," as I explained earlier. This is the dual gravity of our inner nature, the conflict between our desire for self-expansion and our desire for self-contraction; between the superconscious and the subconscious; between the call to perfection and the desire, born of our deeply ingrained habits, to deny any such "highfalutin" pretensions and return to the delusive comfort of our animal origins. These subtler pulls are in opposite directions: toward the upper spine and the brain, and toward the lower parts of the spine and body. The pull downward, relative to our normal upright position, is that of the subconscious. The pull upward is that of superconsciousness.

The subconscious can be conditioned to cooperate with our upward aspirations. In most people, however, attached as they are to their bodies, the subconscious only prolongs their involvement in material desires. Its downward pull, like surrender to the force of gravity, produces relaxation of another kind: the release we experience in surrendering to our animal nature. Such "relaxation" is temporary, and ultimately disappoints every expectation we've ever held of it.

People often justify their surrender to physical desires by pointing with pride to their "liberation" from social conformity. In the end, unfortunately, they pay a great price for their illusive freedom. Living more by the dictates of their subconscious, they find themselves increasingly contractive in their outlook, increasingly centered in their egos, in selfish attitudes, and in their inability to relate to anything that doesn't contribute in some way to their own self-esteem.

To give in to our lower impulses should be viewed, then, not as a release from inner conflict, but as a complete (if temporary) rout. To put the best face on it, it is a "retreat to the rear," as propaganda bulletins from the battle front sometimes put it. This feint, as we may call it, in the direction of failure may be like the temporary freedom a fisherman gives his fish, once it has been caught on the line. He lets it get away temporarily, knowing that if he pulls on his line too hard it may break. By first "playing" the fish, he reels it in safely at last. So be it. Don't ever allow the thought to enter your mind: "I'm beaten." If you do, that will be the end, at least for this incarnation.

The upward pull is opposed only minimally by the earth's gravity—an opposition that can be offset to some extent by standing for a few minutes every day on one's head! This pull is opposed vigorously, however, by the downward pull of the subconscious. To repeat, people who misguidedly seek freedom from this inner tug-of-war by surrendering to downwardness, intending thereby to demonstrate their "rugged self-honesty," are in fact only denying their own best interests, which lie in the higher Self. Such denial is another example of my statement in the last chapter that fact and truth are not always synonyms. Honest admission of our lower nature is not true honesty, for it goes against deeper truths of our own being.

Affirmations of downwardness give emphasis to the delusion that our real place is with our ancestors, the monkeys. To give in completely to our lower nature would imply not only embracing our animal impulses, but descending further still to embrace the relative unconsciousness of the rocks—a goal some people actually strive for in their efforts to deaden their awareness, some by drinking themselves into an alcoholic stupor, others by drugging themselves senseless.

The upward pull of our higher nature is, for most people, weaker than the downward pull, though the call of the soul is eternally persistent, and cannot ultimately be denied. As Paramhansa Yogananda put it in *Autobiography of a Yogi,* "The trivial preoccupations of daily life are not enough for man; wisdom too is a native hunger."

To meditate, it is essential to sit erect with a straight spine. An erect spine aids us in raising our consciousness, permitting the energy to flow freely toward the brain. An erect spine also induces a positive attitude, without which it is easy, in the meditative peace, to sink into subconsciousness.

I once saw an advertisement for a meditation teaching. The "meditator" was leaning back comfortably in a "Lazy Boy" chair. His eyes were closed; his feet, propped up. The teaching that was being promoted can only have been a prescription for mental meandering!

The yoga teachings tell us to eschew idleness. They insist, therefore, on a posture conducive to mental vigor, that at the same time assists in releasing the energy to flow *upward.*

A number of positions are traditionally recommended for meditation. None of them is remotely similar to the illustration in that advertisement, for they all promote an attitude of alertness, of "meaning business" in one's quest for enlightenment. You will find them described in many books on yoga, including one of my own, published in 1967 and still in print: *Yoga Postures for Higher Awareness*.*

The best meditation poses are *siddhasana* (the perfect pose) and *padmasana* (the lotus pose). *Siddhasana* is better suited to the *hatha yogi,* or practitioner of the yoga postures. *Padmasana* is said to be better suited to the *raja yogi,* or practitioner of the yoga science of meditation. The difference in effect between these two poses is slight, but the subtle effect of *siddhasana* tends to be an upward push on the energy from below, whereas that of *padmasana* is to *draw* the energy upward in a spirit of self-offering.

A word about *hatha yoga.* This system, which is thousands of years old, has its basis in Patanjali's third stage or *anga* (limb), called *asana. Hatha yoga* is not a separate yoga path, but is a physical adjunct to *raja yoga,* the yoga of meditation. *Raja yoga* masters give secondary importance to the yoga postures, since *asana* as the third stage of *raja yoga* refers simply to sitting still with a straight spine. *Raja yogis* speak highly of *hatha yoga,* however, as a system that affords great benefits to the body, and also to the mind in its interconnectedness with the body.

Whether or not you yourself practice the *hatha yoga* postures is a personal decision, and depends largely on how much time you have to devote to spiritual practices. Remember only that it is meditation, above all, that will satisfy the needs of your soul.

*Now titled *Ananda Yoga for Higher Awareness* (Nevada City: Crystal Clarity, Publishers, 1994).

The classical yoga positions for meditation are beneficial for several reasons. First, they hold the body steady. Second, they gently press on certain nerves, and thereby help the meditator to achieve physical calmness. Third, they assist in raising the energy toward the brain, and prevent an excessive amount of blood from accumulating in the legs. Finally, they prevent the meditator from falling over during ecstasy, and perhaps getting hurt, as the mind and energy withdraw from body-consciousness.

For Westerners, Paramhansa Yogananda recommended an alternative position. It lacks some of the above benefits, but compensates for this lack by giving meditators, Westerners particularly, a position in which they can relax more easily, without having their attention drawn to the pain in their knees.

1) Sit on a straight-backed, armless chair (you may prefer one with a padded seat), at a height convenient for placing your feet flat on the floor.

2) On the chair, extending onto the floor in front of it and up over the back of the chair, place a woolen blanket. The purpose of the blanket is to insulate your body from certain downward-pulling currents in the earth that are apart from the pull of gravity. If you'd like even better insulation, cover the blanket with a silk cloth.

3) Sit away from the back of the chair. Keep your spine straight, your elbows and shoulders back (drawing the shoulder blades slightly together), and your chin drawn slightly in, parallel to the floor.

4) Place your hands palms upward on the thighs at the junction of the abdomen.

To relax the body, bear in mind that it may hold many knots of tension of which you are not consciously aware. The way to release those lingering tensions is to increase the tension first, deliberately:

1) Inhale. Tense the entire body until it gently vibrates. Then throw the breath out forcibly and relax. Practice this exercise two or three times. Then concentrate deeply on the sense of peace and freedom that permeates your body.

2) Next, for even deeper relaxation, inhale slowly counting mentally to twelve; hold the breath counting to twelve. Exhale again, counting to twelve. Practice this exercise six to twelve times.

This practice can also help us to achieve release from mental and emotional pain. The stress that accompanies such pain usually produces physical tension. By relaxing the body, as outlined above, then extending the thought of physical relaxation to the release of tension in the mind and in the emotions, we can achieve mental and emotional tranquillity with the release of tension in the body.

Whenever you feel anxious or fearful about anything, or distressed over the way someone has treated you, or upset for any reason, inhale and tense the body. Bring your emotions to a focus in the body with that act of tension. Hold the tension briefly, vibrating your emotions along with the body. Throw the breath out, and, keeping the breath exhaled as long as you can do so comfortably, enjoy the feeling of inner peace. Remain for a time without thought.

When the breath returns, or when thoughts once again bestir themselves in your mind, fill your brain with some happy memory that will provide an antidote to your emotions. Concentrate for several minutes on the happiness of that memory.

Throughout this process, look upward, and mentally offer yourself, like a kite, into the winds of inner freedom. Let them sweep you into the skies of superconsciousness.

****

RELAXATION EXERCISE

After practicing the relaxation exercise as described above (tensing and relaxing the body, then taking several deep, slow breaths to a rhythmic count) visualize yourself surrounded by infinite space. Vast emptiness stretches before you—below you—behind—above.

After some time, concentrate on your body. Release into vast space, like thin wisps of vapor, any lingering tension in the muscles.

Release your awareness of the body. It, too, is becoming part of the vast emptiness all around you.

Now, bring that feeling of space upwards in the body—from the feet to the calves, the thighs, the hips and buttocks, the abdomen, the hands, forearms, and upper arms, the back, the chest, the neck and throat, the tongue and lips, the facial muscles, the eyes, the brain, the very top of your head.

This body is no longer yours. You are the essence of which it is but an expression—the subtle consciousness of absolute peace that permeates all things, but that is untouched and unaffected by anything.

Chapter Seven

MEDITATION IS FINDING YOUR CENTER

Meditation teaches you to relate to life and to your environment from who *you* are, not from the way others view you.

The average person is like an eccentric flywheel. I don't mean a flywheel with an offbeat personality, but simply a flywheel that isn't centered properly. The faster the wheel turns, the more violently it vibrates. At a certain speed, its vibration may actually cause it to fly apart.

Most people are frequently in danger of "flying apart," at least mentally. Living at their periphery, not at their center, they vibrate more violently the faster they whirl through life. It is safe to say that few people think of themselves as even *having* a center. They are forever "on edge."

One problem with living at your periphery is that it forces you to relate to other people at theirs. They, in turn, will be "on edge" with you. Your understanding of them, and theirs of you, will be a view from the outside; it will therefore be superficial. As opposed to the concept stated earlier, "center everywhere, circumference nowhere," most people perceive life as "circumference everywhere, center nowhere."

The great ballet dancer Nijinsky had never been on skis when he visited a Swiss ski slope. A ski instructor undertook to show him something of his own skill on skis. Setting off downhill, he made complex leaps and turns as only experts can do. Nijinsky observed him carefully, tuning in as though he himself were skiing. He then duplicated exactly all of the instructor's movements. Amazed, the man simply wouldn't believe that Nijinsky had never been on skis before—that he had never even seen anyone on skis!

The secret of understanding is to get mentally *inside* whatever it is you are trying to understand—to gaze outward, so to speak, from its center rather than inward from its periphery. The secret of understanding other people is to identify with them at their center. To find the center of anything or anyone, first withdraw to your own center and project your feelings empathetically from that point.

Meditation is the process of finding your own center. Techniques exist for doing so, but success depends also to a great extent on holding the right attitudes. Let me first discuss some of those attitudes. Then in the next chapter I'll discuss the techniques.

SELF-ACCEPTANCE

The first attitude fundamental to "centering" is self-acceptance. You are who you are. Make the best of it, and envy no one for what he or she is. Don't draw comparisons between you and others: Encourage yourself, rather, in your efforts to attain *your own* highest potential.

Self-acceptance will come progressively as you try to live up to the highest that is in you. Unless you are already in superconsciousness, you cannot but recognize the fact that an inner conflict exists between your soul's call to the heights, and the siren call of temptation to the depths. You can't laugh off soul-longing, though you may try.

Soul-conscience is not something imposed on us from without. It rises spontaneously from within ourselves. Often in history, soul-conscience has pitted individuals *against* society—it brought Jesus Christ to the cross, and Socrates to the poisonous cup of hemlock.

Hamlet's mother said, "The lady doth protest too much, methinks." One might as justifiably say, "That person doth laugh too much, methinks." Be careful, if ever you find yourself making too much fun of anything or anyone. What you denounce in others is a clue to the faults you have in yourself. Make sure, then, that you are not merely hiding from some failing in yourself.

True conscience is innate. It is the silent voice of the soul. To achieve self-acceptance, you must be clear in your true conscience. Such clarity comes only when we accept that our higher Self is our eternal reality.

Needless to say, one doesn't achieve this degree of self-acceptance in a single leap. So long as you sincerely resist your lower impulses, and strive toward your own inner heights, your conscience will be reasonably clear, and you will find yourself able to achieve that measure of emotional and psychic relaxation without which it is not possible to find rest at one's center.

Self-acceptance makes it possible for one to view others also in their own higher nature, and to accept that potential as their own reality. Only from within will it ever be possible for you to know others truly. When you relate to their center from your own, you will find that they, too, respond to you from that center in themselves. Soul speaks to soul, and recognizes itself in an infinity of manifestations. This was what Jesus meant by the words "Love thy neighbor as thyself."

My guru, Paramhansa Yogananda, lived always at that center. Wherever he went, he attracted utter strangers to himself. Friends of mine a few years ago stopped at a gas station. The attendant, an older man, recognized a photograph of Yogananda on the dashboard of their car as he was cleaning the windshield. Deeply moved, he related how "that man"—about whom he apparently knew little or nothing—would stop for gas at a station in Highland Park where he had once worked. That contact, casual though it was, had had a profound effect on his life.

When it comes to understanding things rather than people at their center, as Nijinsky did during his observation of the ski instructor, you will find the doors of innumerable mysteries unlocking themselves for you. Any undertaking, indeed, to which you apply your mind will come out successfully.

I've tested this principle many times, and in many ways. It is no abstraction, nor is it a question of individual talent. It is, simply, a practical application of the truth, "center everywhere, circumference nowhere."

KINDNESS

Acceptance leads to the second attitude necessary for finding your own center: *kindness*. To achieve that clarity of conscience which is the companion of self-acceptance, you should practice kindness also toward yourself. You'll never overcome your failings by hating your shortcomings, nor by hating yourself for indulging in them. Of course, you shouldn't allow kindness to *excuse* them. In true kindness to yourself, you should work, rather, to strengthen yourself in virtue. Seek always your own highest potentials. If this means being stern with yourself occasionally, so be it. But never be judgmental.

Kindness is necessary also for understanding other people. In fact, without it, there can never be acceptance of them. By kind acceptance you will find yourself intuitively aware of them at their center.

Kind acceptance may be a more difficult concept to visualize in connection with inanimate things. As a means of achieving such understanding, relaxed acceptance rather than kindness may be an easier concept to grasp. And yet, because consciousness is inherent in all things, to feel kindness toward things also need not really strain the point.

ATTUNEMENT

As a young man Paramhansa Yogananda commissioned a well-known artist in Bengal to paint a portrait of his guru's guru, Lahiri Mahasaya. The artist did a competent job, but his painting lacked intuitive perception of his subject. Yogananda asked him, "How long did it take you to master your art?"

"Twenty years," was the reply.

"You mean it took you twenty years to convince yourself you could paint?" the yogi inquired. The query came as a shock to the artist.

"Why, I'd like to see you paint as well in twice that length of time!" he exclaimed indignantly.

"Give me a week," Yogananda replied. The artist, angered by what he imagined to have been meant as an insult, left the room.

Yogananda had no practical knowledge of painting. His first attempts were unsuccessful. As he persevered, however, he tuned in more and more deeply to the understanding that is required of an artist. By the end of that week, his painting was finished. The artist, on beholding it, had to admit it was much better than his own.

The more you attune yourself from your center to the center in everything, the more you will find that there is a sympathetic inter-relationship in the universe that makes possible the perfect understanding of all things. Depend not on intellectual analysis, which separates things and compartmentalizes them, but try to *feel* the heart of whatever it is you are trying to understand.

Friends of mine in India were once climbing in the Almora district of the Himalayas. On a high plateau they encountered a hermit who rarely saw other human beings. When this man, who was uneducated, realized that my friends weren't able to converse with him in his native dialect, he spoke to them fluently in English.

Anandamoyee Ma, a saint with whom I spent some time in India, was illiterate. But if scholars asked her to explain some difficult or obscure scriptural text, she would do so to their full satisfaction. All she asked was that someone read it to her first. She once told me, "I could speak English, if I concentrated on it." She went on to say a few words in English, laughing merrily as she did so.

Paramhansa Yogananda could converse easily with people of specialized knowledge, such as physicians, using their own terminology as though he'd been to medical school himself. As another example, a lady in Mexico City who spoke no English had a private interview for one hour with Yogananda, who spoke no Spanish. "I don't know how it happened," she told me years later, "but we understood each other perfectly."

A Process of Unlearning

Finding your own center, then, is not a process of divorcing yourself from objective reality, but of touching that universal center of which all objective reality is a manifestation. To do so bestows far greater than normal comprehension. And this comprehension differs radically from the usual understanding gleaned from superficial facts and observations. Wisdom gained from tuning in to one's own center is not at all like going to school, where the goal is to learn. Meditation is a process of *unlearning*.

I don't mean that we should try to forget all the knowledge we acquired at school. That knowledge has its place, and its own usefulness. Meditation, moreover, is not a path to intellectual ineptitude: Quite the contrary, it greatly sharpens the intellect. What we must "unlearn," instead, are the limitations of delusion imposed on us by our egos.

"I'm a man"; "I'm a woman"; "I'm an American, a Frenchman, an Italian"; "I like modern art"; "I like climbing mountains"; "I hate Baroque music." Rudolph Fleish wrote of a woman he'd once met who insisted, "I've no use for Brooklyn dentists!" Self-limiting ideas such as these enclose us in a cocoon of spiritual ignorance—we, who in our deeper reality are the eternal Spirit! The process of unlearning takes us to deeper and deeper levels of self-recognition.

Neti, neti—"not this, not that." Unlearning is a process of eradicating every false notion from the mind. It means getting back to what and *where* we really are: not "out there"; not ensconced in a little body—male or female, white or black, Mexican or American—but *here*, at our own eternal center, no matter where the body happens to be.

An English lady once visited the sage Ramana Maharshi, in India. "I've come here all the way from London," she announced, "just to find you."

"You haven't moved at all," was his reply. "Your view of the world has simply changed."

As far as our own perceptions are concerned, we are forever at the center of the universe. There is no circumference to these perceptions, except as we ourselves draw them. Our superconscious center is everywhere. Whether consciously or not (much more so, however, if we do it consciously) our influence extends outward into our environment. And our environment, in its turn, exerts a reciprocal influence upon us. Meditation not only enables us to "tune in" more sensitively to our environment, but also to harmonize ourselves with it, and it with us.

COOPERATING WITH MAGNETIC
INFLUENCES

Scientists have been discovering increasingly that we live in an electromagnetic universe. This is a very different view from that held a scant century ago, when the universe seemed to be entirely material.

Magnetism is generated by the flow of many kinds of energy, not only of electricity. There are subtler energies, and subtler forms of magnetism, than those measurable by any physical instrument. Paramhansa Yogananda described electricity as "the animal current in the energy world." Energy is present in physical locations. Places develop magnetism according to the thoughts and subtle energies of the people who have frequented them. Visitors can feel these vibrations.

It is relatively easy to feel the uplifting atmosphere in a temple or a church, for example, where people have worshiped with devotion. Such vibrations are even stronger in places where great saints have meditated. On the other hand, one can sense discordant vibrations, also, in low "dives" of the type frequented by sailors on shore leave.

You will find it easier to meditate in places that are suffused with spiritually uplifting vibrations. You can create such a place in your own home, by setting aside one room purely for meditation, or even by screening off a portion of your bedroom. If you restrict your use of that area to meditation, you will discover, in a few months, that it has developed vibrations that will raise you quickly into a meditative mood.

Less obviously, spiritual vibrations also permeate things that are insubstantial, such as prayers that have been uttered, and chants that have been sung, by great saints or by devout worshipers for many years. If, at the beginning of your meditation, you repeat such prayers or chants, you will find that they have the power to lift you into a state of inner communion. "Chanting," Yogananda used to say, "is half the battle."

I will go more deeply into the subject of chanting in another chapter. For now, let us limit our discussion to the importance of attuning ourselves to the vibrations that are part of the very atmosphere of this planet on which we live.

The yogis of India endorse a tradition that one encounters in many cultures and traditions around the world. The Navajo, for example, build their hogans, and the Sioux their teepees, with the entrances facing east. From this direction, according to them, "all good things come." The archaic Hebrew word for east is *kedem*, from the same root as "before." The idea is that one should pray facing the east. Yogis, similarly, recommend facing eastward during meditation.

For the earth itself generates a powerful magnetic field. The direction faced in meditation has an effect on what we might call the electromagnetism of our bodies.

The most spiritually beneficial rays come from the east. From the north come rays that promote a consciousness of inner freedom. Traditionally, north is the best direction to face for leaving the body consciously at death.

I don't mean to suggest that you can't meditate effectively facing in any direction that is convenient for you. The traditionally recommended directions are aids, only. A strong will can rise above any external influence. The will is assisted, however, by supportive influences, so why not take advantage of them?

The flow of civilization itself is from east to west. A greater spirit of freedom resides in the northern part of every country, and a spirit of faithfulness to tradition in the southern part. There are countless connections between the earth's magnetism and our own.

To harmonize ourselves with the earth's energies, it is good also to meditate at special hours of the day. The magnetism of Earth, relative to our position on the planet, changes perceptibly at different times. These times are when the sun crosses the horizon at sunrise and at sunset, and when it is at its highest and lowest points, at noon and at midnight.

Let me digress a little here. Superconsciousness has its bodily center in the frontal lobe of the brain. The conscious state operates from the middle part of the brain; the subconscious, from the lower brain. Thus, there is a kind of linear progression of awareness from subconsciousness toward superconsciousness.

In another sense, however, superconsciousness exists *between* the conscious and subconscious states—not in its physical center in the brain, but in the subtle way it functions. That is to say, because both the superconscious and the subconscious induce mental peace—much more intensely so, of course, in the case of superconsciousness—there is an interchange between them. Superconscious inspirations often reach us during sleep, through the subconscious; they are often more difficult to receive during our conscious, more active state. Truth ultimately, like space itself, is spherical, not linear. That is why opposites so often resemble each other. In this sense there is a link also, or a resemblance, between superconsciousness and subconsciousness.

Superconsciousness has been described as residing at a fine dividing line between the conscious and subconscious minds. For this reason yogis recommend meditating on the horizon where it forms a straight line, such as you see especially when you gaze out at the sea. If you can mentally penetrate that line, you will enter superconsciousness.

We might put it this way: Physically, we live in a three-dimensional universe. If we can reduce those three dimensions to one—the straight horizon, or the straight line formed by the eyebrows—and gaze at that line intently, it is easier to penetrate *beyond* this three-dimensional world and enter the divine world, which has no dimensions.

Similarly, if we can catch the rest point between two breaths, or the rest points in nature when the sun changes its direction relative to the earth, or to our position on the earth, it is easier for us to penetrate beyond this three-dimensional world into superconsciousness.

The best times of the day for meditation are six a.m. (sunrise), noon (when the sun is at zenith), six p.m. (sunset), and midnight (when the sun is at its nadir). The best times in the year to meditate, from this perspective, are at the equinoxes (March 21 and September 21, approximately) and the solstices (June 21 and December 21, approximately).

You should also consider your own convenience, however. Modern life is not always easily adapted to Nature's broader rhythms.

It is good to meditate, however briefly, on first awaking in the morning, or at least to say a short prayer at that time. The subconscious mind is more open to suggestion during that brief span of time when we are rising up the shaft of consciousness to wakefulness. The same is true, in reverse, as we fall asleep at night, as the mind slips down again into subconsciousness. On waking, the subconscious stands ready to resume its task of influencing the conscious mind in its decisions. That is why we describe someone who seems grumpy by saying "He must have got up on the wrong side of bed this morning." At the moment of waking, a strong affirmation of will can completely change the direction of subconscious influence on the mind.

Again, as we slip down into sleep at night we can carry into the subconscious the thoughts and resolutions of the conscious mind. It is these which are likely to be uppermost in the subconscious when we awake the following morning. Thus, if a person falls asleep with the thought "I'm utterly exhausted!" he may well feel just as exhausted when he wakes in the morning.

But he will wake up alert and ready for action if, while falling asleep the night before, he tells himself, "I'll do my duty to the body by giving it the rest it needs, but tomorrow morning I'll be wide awake and ready!"

Meditate before going to bed. Then, as you fall asleep, take the meditative peace with you.

Another thing to do, just as you are on the point of falling asleep, is try to catch the moment *between* wakefulness and sleep, and slip gently into semi-superconsciousness.

It is best to meditate on an empty stomach, or at least an hour or two after a heavy meal. It will be easier to direct the energy upward if it is not being kept busy digesting food.

A final point: Meditate, as much as possible, at the same hours daily. Your subconscious will cooperate better with your efforts to achieve calmness in meditation, once it accepts the habit of putting aside distractions at those hours.

****

MEDITATION EXERCISE

Develop the ability to pass at will from one state of consciousness to another. A helpful practice in this regard is to ally your state of consciousness with the position of your eyes.

You will find, when you look down, that the mind tends more easily to drift into subconsciousness. When you look straight ahead, it is easier to shake off sleep's lethargy. And when you look up, it is easier to soar up into higher consciousness and to feel inspiration.

Practice this exercise:

1) Look down, closing your eyes. Feel yourself drifting downward as if sinking through water—through forests of waving seaweed—ever deeper into a green, misty world of fantasy. Enjoy this pleasant sense of freedom from earthly responsibility, from demanding projects, from fears, from worldly ambitions. Affirm mentally, "Through slowly drifting waters, I sink into subconsciousness."

2) Now, with a quick burst of will power, open your eyes and gaze straight ahead. Shake off the last clinging tendrils of passivity. Affirm, "With a burst of energy I rise to greet the world!"

3) Remain in that state a few moments. Then look upward and affirm, "I awake in Thy light! I am joyful! I am free! I awake in Thy light!"

Practice alternating between these three states of consciousness, accompanying them with a corresponding shift in the position of your eyes. Gradually, you will gain the ability to control your states of consciousness at will.

Chapter Eight

LOCATING YOUR CENTER

The great master Sri Ramakrishna gave to the world a wonderful image of spiritual progress. "What remains," he asked, "when you peel an onion? Nothing! An onion consists of peels. Similarly, when you peel away the layers of delusion from the mind, what is left? Nothing material. Nothing mental or psychological. All that is left is pure consciousness."

The "peels" he described begin with matter in its grossest state. Evolution is a process of gradually stripping away the peels enclosing the Spirit in its material manifestations. The Indian writings use the word *kosha* (sheath). Until the outermost *kosha* is removed, pure consciousness is so densely covered that it appears unconscious. Thus we have its appearance of insensibility in the rocks and metals. Gradually, through upward evolution, one sheath after another is removed. In human beings, only a few sheaths remain. They too must be stripped away—not by the automatic process of evolution, but by deliberate refinement of the heart's feelings through devotion and by the power of will.

The emotions must be refined to pure intuitive feeling. The thoughts must be refined to calm intuitive wisdom. Desires for sense enjoyments must be refined to absorption in inner, spiritual lights, sounds, and similar counterparts to the other physical senses.

From a practical point of view, what the meditator comes to realize is that he doesn't need to reach outside himself for divine succor. All he needs is to remove the coatings that cover his consciousness, and that protect his ego from the staggering challenge of omnipresence while comforting him with the delusion of his egoic self-sufficiency.

There are two aspects to the spiritual path. One of them is abstract and philosophical; the other, concrete and practical. Both are important for understanding this subject properly.

From a philosophical perspective, what is left after the peeling process ends is—nothing! It is like extinguishing a candle, except that, in the case of a candle, the wick—that is to say, the ego—still remains, and can therefore be lit once again. In the shedding of the final *kosha* there is no ego left to be reactivated. This is *nirvana*. It is the goal of all meditation practice, understood variously by the followers of the different religions.

When great masters are born in this world, they teach according to the spiritual needs and readiness of the people of their times. What generally happens, later on, is that the disciples—most of whom, in varying measure, fall short of the attainment of full enlightenment—give a new emphasis to those teachings. Desirous of demonstrating the uniqueness of those teachings, and therefore not so bent on addressing the spiritual needs of their times, they seize upon one aspect or another of his teachings with a view to highlighting those aspects which seem to set his teachings apart from those of other teachers. Because the spiritual path deals with many levels of reality that are too subtle for sensory observation, they will argue heatedly over points that neither they nor their listeners have any way of proving or disproving. Thus, they pass from carefully intellectualized dogmas to dogmatism, from dogmatism to bigotry, and from bigotry to persecution, each fully convinced that his own teacher alone knew the truth.

Meanwhile, those teachers are probably "in some corner of the hubbub coucht,"* sipping tea together in perfect amity.

During the course of a relatively long life, I've discovered a formula that seems to work very well, no matter where you apply it: *Dogmatism increases in direct proportion to a person's inability to prove his point.*

---

*From *The Rubaiyat of Omar Khayyam,* Quatrain Forty-Five of the first edition. Paramhansa Yogananda wrote in his commentary on this quatrain in *The Rubaiyat of Omar Khayyam Explained* (Nevada City, CA: Crystal Clarity, Publishers, 1994):

"When people first start out on the search for truth, their quest, often, is merely intellectual. They pride themselves on the subtlety of their reasoning, and see not how like their theories are to bubbles blown on a breeze, held briefly together by the surface tension of their unproved convictions.

"Every theory, ardently espoused, is at odds with every other. Each noisily attracts customers to its booth by vaunting its own brilliance and originality. It is an exciting game at first, as the ego runs eagerly in passionate pursuit of one bubble after another. At last, however, nothing lingers in the mind but spiritual doubt and confusion."

Nirvana

The Buddhist (not necessarily the Buddha's) concept of *nirvana* is total extinction, not only of the candle flame (desires and attachments) and the wick (the ego), but of the candle (that is to say, consciousness) itself. Thus, their teaching is in many ways identical to the philosophy of Descartes, to whom consciousness was a product of thinking ("I think, therefore I am"). The difference between the two is only that Buddhists point out, quite rightly, that much more defines our existence than the mere act of thinking.

If the goal of spiritual endeavor were to extinguish consciousness itself, one might ask, What differentiates spiritual practices from suicide? The only thing wrong with suicide, from this point of view, is that it doesn't bestow complete annihilation. Unfulfilled desires remain as *vrittis* (vortices of consciousness and energy) in the astral body even after death, and cause the soul to reincarnate again and again, going through the whole weary process that led to the decision to kill oneself in the first place. Thus, we are led—by what amounts, as we shall see, to a fundamental misunderstanding of the concept—to the conclusion that *nirvana* is better than suicide for one reason only: *Nirvana* works, whereas suicide botches the job.

Shall we think of *nirvana,* then, in the terms suggested by the way its proponents explain it: as a kind of permanent suicide—the permanence that suicide cases themselves desire, but fail to achieve? It is the example of Buddha himself that has kept people from making this analogy. He was so obviously not a potential suicide case. But then, that only means that people have misunderstood what he meant by *nirvana*. Having come this far with our analogy, then, let us be no longer abstract about it, but let us look at suicide itself.

Nirvana is a concept far beyond normal human comprehension. It can be dogmatized about at length without fear of contradiction, except on equally dogmatic grounds. Suicide, however, is something we all know about. If we don't fully understand the reasons for it, we've at least known people, or known of people, who shocked everyone by killing themselves.

It is safe to say that nothing about their zeal for self-destruction inspires emulation. If *successful* suicide, as opposed to botching the job, were the true goal of spirituality, it would be difficult to imagine anyone devoting more than token effort to spiritual practices.

In fact, however, Buddhism inspires people not by its invitation to non-existence—an invitation usually accepted, one suspects, with the Buddhist equivalent of asking for a rain check—but because of the positive qualities the Buddha himself manifested: compassion, calmness, acceptance, to name only a few. All of these qualities enable a person to cope *more consciously* with life; they in no way inspire such negative attitudes as might reduce one to huddling morosely in a basement, contemplating self-annihilation.

Buddhism is a great religion. *Nirvana* is a great concept. Loyalty, moreover, is a great virtue. Buddhists demonstrate the greatness of their religion by the qualities they develop by following it sincerely: compassion, non-attachment, and calmness, again to name only a

117

few. When it comes to their understanding of *nirvana,* however, and to their opposition of that concept to the stated goals of other religions, we must answer that truth either exists or it doesn't. If it exists, there cannot be differences of opinion regarding it. Among great masters in all religions who have realized that truth—again, assuming the truth exists—there *has* to be fundamental unanimity. Whatever differences exist can only do so in matters of emphasis.

In their outer lives, which is the only part of them that others can readily observe, those great masters have all demonstrated the same characteristics of spiritual greatness: compassion, universal love, kindness, forgiveness, calmness, understanding. None of them has ever set his own teachings above or against the teachings of other great masters. The only concepts any of them has opposed are spiritual misinterpretations of those teachings—the confusion created in spiritual teaching, in other words, by unenlightened people.

It is the tendency of spiritually ignorant humanity to scour the great teachings of the ages for points of disagreement. This is because the intellect's way of arriving at understanding is to analyze and to separate concepts from one another. The right method of understanding in these matters, however, is with calm intuitive feeling. Sri Rama Yogi, a great saint in India, brought me up sharp on this point. He had made a statement to which I'd replied, "That isn't what my guru taught."

With a slight smile he replied: "If all the disciples of great saints fully understood their masters, there wouldn't be the fighting that one sees in religion everywhere!"

The intellect can serve us well for *explaining* a truth. The truth itself, however, must first be perceived by intuition. Thus has it ever been, even in the physical sciences.

To return, then, to the concept of *nirvana:* The Buddha was not counseling self-destruction. The release that he taught from the sorrows of life and death was offered, rather, in terms of self-*fulfillment.* Nirvana is a universal truth. It is not the unique discovery of one great soul in history. The very word *nirvana* was known and accepted long before Buddha's time. It was not his discovery of this truth that made him great, but his perfect *attainment* of it.

Nirvana is Pure Consciousness, that state which remains after the process of removing sheath after sheath of delusive self-identity has been completed. Once the onion has been completely peeled, nothing is left of it *as a physical object.* Once the *kosha*s have been completely removed, nothing is left that one can call individuality—no body, no emotions, no desires, thoughts, or attachments. Not even the ego remains, though even when that is gone there are still waves of feeling to be calmed. Everything is extinguished, like the flame of a candle. The wick of ego is destroyed. What is left? Existence cannot have appeared out of non-existence. Things manifest cannot have appeared literally out of nothing. The very compassion of the Buddha, and of practicing Buddhists, each according to his own ability, cannot have been the product of unawareness. The "nothingness" of *nirvana,* then, is a state of being, and has often been so described. It is not a *non*-state.

What happens, as my guru explained, is that in that "nothingness" one realizes, "I have been stripped of every self-definition: Yet I exist!" In this state is experienced, at first, a certain bereavement—the last attempt by the subconscious to draw the mind back into human consciousness. If the meditator resists that final temptation, as the Buddha did with his declaration, "*Mara* [death, or Satanic delusion], I have conquered thee!" he suddenly finds bursting upon his consciousness wave upon cosmic wave of bliss.

This is the very definition of God, *Satchidananda:* "Ever-existing, ever-conscious, ever-new Bliss." It was from this state of awareness that the Buddha was able so perfectly to express the quality of compassion. The same universal love was demonstrated by Jesus Christ. It was demonstrated by every other great master who ever lived, each in his or her way: For every soul—indeed, every atom in the universe—is uniquely itself.

I shall return to this teaching later on, approaching it from a direction that may be easier to understand in terms of normal human experience. For now, our discussion concerns locating our inner center.

From a philosophical standpoint, it may be asked, "Center of what, if nothing really exists?" Yogananda's explanation, "Center everywhere, circumference nowhere," works wonderfully in a more philosophical context, but it is difficult to objectify in a concrete model. Such a model does exist, however. We have only to take a more down-to-earth approach to the subject and ask, "How can I locate my center in this physical body?" *Have* we, in fact, a physical center?

THE SPINE IS THE CENTER

The whole path of meditation, and of yoga practice specifically, begins with awareness of the body and uses bodily awareness as a guide to help us to transcend physical limitations.

There are four basic aspects of consciousness: mind (*mon*), intellect (*buddhi*), ego (*ahankara*), and feeling (*chitta*). Paramhansa Yogananda described them thus:

The mind is like a mirror. It reflects, simply, whatever is placed before it.

The intellect defines what it sees reflected in the mirror. If the reflection is of a horse, the intellect determines, impersonally, "That's a horse."

The ego then personalizes what it sees in the mirror by declaring, "That's *my* horse!"

Feeling, then—in Sanskrit, *chitta*—strengthens the bond of involvement by declaring, "How happy I am to see my horse!"

It is *chitta* that ties the knot, so to speak, in the rope of delusive involvement.

Mind is centered at the top of the head; the intellect, in the frontal lobe of the brain at a point midway between the eyebrows; the ego, in the medulla oblongata at the base of the brain; feeling, in the region of the spine opposite the heart. Human consciousness, more generally speaking, is centered all along the spine.

Some of these points are easily corroborated by our everyday experience. Whenever we think deeply, for instance, we tend to knit the eyebrows (the seat of the intellect). Often, too, we'll look upward—one more indication that our consciousness is focused there.

121

Again, whenever we feel a strong emotion, it's in the heart that we feel it. People who have been disappointed in love are prone to say, "I'm heartbroken!" I can't imagine anyone crying, "She's left me! Ah, how my knees ache!" It is in the heart—or, rather, in the spine in the heart region—that we experience emotional pain.

The medulla oblongata is more difficult to relate to the ego in terms of common experience, but a little reflection makes the connection. Simply observe common human gestures. When people express pride, for example, they draw their heads back—indicating tension in the back of the neck around the medulla. The popular description for such a person is: "He's looking down his nose."

Again, when people feel flattered, they have a tendency to move their heads slightly from side to side, as though waves of pleasure were passing through the medulla.

It is from the location of the medulla, Yogananda explained, that the sperm and ovum, when united, move outward to create the physical body. The energy, as it creates the body, moves upward from the medulla to the brain, and downward from the medulla through the spinal column, whence it radiates outward to form the nervous system and the body. The medulla oblongata is the seat of life in the body, and contains the only body part that cannot be operated on, except peripherally.

The spine is the center of the body. The ego is the center of body-consciousness. Various spiritual teachings recommend concentrating in different places along the spine, but all of them in one way or another relate to the spine as the center from which spiritual practice begins.

Christian writers often teach people to meditate in the heart. This is because the feeling quality is centered in the spine, opposite the heart.

Zen Buddhists often teach people to meditate in the area of the navel. This, again, is because there is an important psychic center in the spine opposite the navel.

Why these differences, one may ask, if the truth is one? It is indeed one, but it can be approached in various ways, and with different purposes, according to the temperament and particular needs of the times, and of the individual practitioners.

****

MEDITATION EXERCISE

Sit upright, away from the back of your chair (unless you are sitting on the floor).

Concentrate in the spine. Remember, the spine is not your backbone (those knobs that you feel along the back). It runs more or less through the center of your body. Feel that as your center.

Sway the body left and right. Feel a resistance to that movement in the spine—as though you were perfectly still at your own center.

Now, feel yourself breathing in the spine: up with every inhalation, down with every exhalation. Let the movement begin in the region of the heart, starting at a point slightly below it and extending slightly above.

Lengthen the flow gradually, beginning lower in the spine and ending higher up.

At last, take a slow, deep breath through the nostrils, beginning at the base of the spine and ending at the point between the eyebrows. Hold the breath at that point as long as it is comfortable to do so.

This time, with your exhalation, feel your breath and consciousness soaring out through the forehead, taking you with them into infinite space.

Concentrate, now, on infinity. Feel that from your own center all things are cognizable.

Chapter Nine

WHERE TO CONCENTRATE

Live more in the spine. There lies the battlefield where the inner forces of light and darkness are engaged in the struggle for final victory. The outcome of this war is predestined, for you are a child of the light, not of darkness. It can be delayed indefinitely, however, for the struggle to transcend darkness will last as long as you yourself allow it to.

Why delay indefinitely, however, suffering endless pains and disappointments? As Sri Krishna urged in the *Bhagavad Gita,* "Get away, O Arjuna, from this ocean of suffering and misery!"*

---

*I've mentioned the *Bhagavad Gita* (Lord's Song) before. The popularity of this scripture is well justified, for no other text so clearly and beautifully expresses the essence of the far more ancient scriptures, the *Vedas.* The language of the *Vedas,* owing to their extreme antiquity, is often so abstruse that few scholars, even, have been able to penetrate its mysteries. Many of the words have changed so greatly in meaning that the significance of whole passages has been lost. To have faith in the authority of the *Vedas* today requires faith, first, in the testimonial of great masters, particularly those who lived close to those times and who were familiar with the ancient modes of expression. One such teacher was the *adhi* (first) Swami Shankaracharya. His praise of those scriptures goes a long way

The inner struggle, as I explained earlier, takes place between the pull of the soul from above, and that of matter and material involvement from below. The spine

toward refuting modern scholars who see in the *Veda*s only rustic hymns depicting a tribal way of life.

Swami Bharati Krishna Tirtha, the *Jagadguru Shankaracharya* (a spiritual descendant of *adhi* Shankaracharya) of Gowardhan Math, a man accepted by many as the supreme authority within Hindu orthodoxy, stated that it was only after a prolonged study of ancient lexicons that he was able to unravel the meaning of certain texts in the *Veda*s relating to mathematics. The swami himself was also a mathematician, and was deeply interested in what the *Veda*s had to say on the subject. Yet the text before him posed seemingly insurmountable difficulties.

"In the reign of King Kamsa," it said, "there was famine, pestilence, and bloodshed." (This is an approximation of the quote; I do not recall it exactly.) What on earth, he wondered, could these words have to do with mathematics? Then he discovered archaic meanings that clarified the passage and showed it actually to be a highly sophisticated mathematical formula.

Sri Aurobindo, a saint of modern India, discovered during a similar study that the word "cow" in the *Veda*s didn't refer to cows at all, but to the spiritual light. "Horses," similarly, was a reference to spiritual power. Both words had acquired secondary meanings, and subsequently had lost their first meanings.

A story is told in the *Veda*s of a certain young man (thus the story reads in modern editions) who was instructed by his guru, to whom he'd gone for initiation, to go off by himself with a small herd of cattle. When the size of the herd had increased sufficiently, he was to return and receive enlightenment.

The actual meaning of the story is that when the young man went to his guru, the guru initiated him into the inner light. He then told the disciple to go off by himself and increase the strength of that light by deepening meditation until he was ready for full initiation and enlightenment. At that time, he was to return to the guru for the touch of ecstasy.

is a long downward extension of the subconscious. At the base of the spine, the outward-flowing energy becomes locked at its south pole, where it is referred to as *kundalini*. The north pole is at the top of the cranium, where it is referred to as the *sahasrara* (thousand-petaled lotus). (St. Teresa of Avila wrote that, according to her inner experiences, the seat of the soul is at the top of the head.)

Every unfulfilled desire, every wave of like or dislike, every karmic action creates a subtle vortex of energy, which the ego spins around itself. They are held together by the centripetal thought: "I want this; I reject that; I like this; I don't like that; This is what I have done; That is what I failed to accomplish." The ego hugs these thoughts and impulses to itself until they gain release outwardly in action, or inwardly in Self-realization. To work out a desire or a karma in the outer world is, ultimately, not feasible, for out of every fulfilled desire there arise two, or twenty, or a hundred others. This is the inner significance of the Greek legend of the Hydra, the many-headed serpent that Hercules slew. The mythical monster would grow two heads for every one that was cut off.

The *vrittis*, or vortices, enter the subconscious and sink to their respective levels in the spine, according to the relative grossness or refinement of the energy they express. A powerful energy, generated by an intense involvement of the will, creates a similarly dynamic vortex. Very old vortices, as yet unresolved, are submerged, so to speak, by more recently created vortices, and have little or no effect on the waking consciousness.

127

They continue, however, like little ripples on the surface of larger waves, to obscure the clear reflection of the Eternal Spirit until long after the larger waves of *chitta*, or intuitive feeling, have subsided. For each vortex, even the oldest and least active, represents a commitment of energy on the part of the will, even if long ago and forgotten. This explains why some people find it difficult to rise above bodily awareness even when they strive their very best to grow spiritually. There are countless such vortices, not even taking into account the possibility that we may have incarnated before in other bodies, each incarnation producing its own nest of *vritti*s.

THE ASTRAL BODY

How, people wonder, is it possible for so many vortices of energy to coexist in the limited space of one spine? There are two answers to this question. One is that our bodies are by no means so little as they seem, relative to everything else in the universe. In a scale of size from the largest heavenly body to the tiniest atom, the size of the human body is approximately half-way.

The other answer is that when the ancient texts describe energies in the body they refer to subtle forces, which displace nothing in the material realm. Behind the physical body, as I've intimated earlier, there is an astral body of energy, on the pattern of which the physical body is created. The vortices of energy in the spine reside primarily in this astral body. Most of the energies awakened through meditation practices are experienced in the astral body.

Yogananda defined the ego as "the soul attached to the body." This attachment begins with the creation of the astral, not of the physical, body. At physical death we leave our material bodies, but keep their astral counterpart intact, with its consciousness of "I" as a separate and discrete reality. The ego forms the vortex of energy that holds the astral body together.

I said earlier that the seat of the intellect is the frontal lobe of the brain, and, more specifically, the point between the eyebrows. I was referring more to astral energies, however, as they manifest themselves through the physical brain. In fact, concentration at that point stimulates levels of awareness that are far higher than intellectual. For this is the seat of ecstasy and spiritual vision in the body. That is why saints have been observed gazing upward during prayer or meditation, and are often so depicted in paintings.

The point between the eyebrows, then, is the best place to concentrate in meditation. The spine is the channel through which the energy is directed to that point.

THE SPIRITUAL EYE

The medulla is the seat of ego in the body. It is the negative pole of Self-consciousness. The positive pole is located at the point between the eyebrows. Here is the center of the higher expression of Self-consciousness. At this point is beheld also the Spiritual Eye, which is a reflection of the energy that enters the body constantly from the surrounding universe, through the medulla.

The Spiritual Eye is not imaginary. It is something one actually sees in meditation, when the thoughts are stilled, and when the intellect functions on its own higher, intuitive level. Many that I've met have told me they'd seen the Spiritual Eye in meditation, some of them long before they had any idea what it was. Some saw it even before they knew about the spiritual path.

When the Spiritual Eye is beheld clearly, it is a golden circle of light surrounding a field of deep blue. In the center of this blue field is a white star with five points. When the Spiritual Eye is beheld imperfectly, it is seen as a dim violet light with a faint circle around it, and an even fainter dot in the center.

Whether or not you behold the Spiritual Eye, by meditating at that point your consciousness will gradually rise until at last it passes the portals of human awareness and enters the state of ecstasy, or superconsciousness.

To concentrate at the point between the eyebrows, look upward—not crossing your eyes, but converging them slightly as though you were gazing at your thumbnail outstretched above you. The important thing is that your *attention,* not your eyes, be focused on that point in the forehead. Don't try forcibly to bring your eyes to a focus, but gaze mentally at that point, and let the Spiritual Eye draw you into itself.

One problem people face is not knowing from what position, mentally, to approach that spiritual center. Lahiri Mahasaya, my guru's spiritual grandfather (his guru's guru), said to concentrate the attention first in the region of the medulla oblongata, and from that point to gaze toward the Spiritual Eye. People's awareness of their egos is often distributed vaguely throughout the body. By centering it consciously in its true seat, the medulla, it becomes possible to direct ego-consciousness toward its own higher octave.

Once ego-consciousness has been dissolved in super-consciousness, the center of consciousness shifts naturally from the ego to the heart. At this point, intuitive feeling takes one's consciousness upward through the Spiritual Eye and out into Infinity.

The Subtle Bodily Energies

Scientists, as I said earlier, are finding more and more that we live in an electromagnetic universe. Science has taken little account of the body's magnetism, for the reason that modern instruments either can't measure it, or get such a weak signal that it seems insignificant. X-rays used to be considered innocuous for the same reason. In fact, the subtle bodily energies are both powerful and important. The reason they appear weak compared to electricity can be explained by the analogy of the radio: If a radio is not perfectly tuned to the station you want, the signal will be weak or distorted. Modern instruments, similarly, tuned as they are to grosser frequencies of electric energy, are unable to pick up the signals of subtle frequencies. Nevertheless, the flow of energy in the body is, in its own way, more powerful than electricity, even as the subtler aspects of matter itself have power over the grosser. (By exploding the atom, more power is generated than by exploding dynamite.)

Wherever there is a flow of electricity, a magnetic field is generated. The stronger the flow, the stronger also the field. In the body also, a strong flow of energy generates a strong magnetic field. It is common knowledge that certain people emit powerful magnetism—some of them in an uplifting way; others, because of their strongly negative energy, in a way that pulls others down. People whose will power and energy are weak emit very little magnetism. Magnetism is closely related to these two factors: will power and energy.

I will discuss later a technique for generating spiritual magnetism. Meanwhile, I touch on this subject here because it relates in an important way to the *vrittis* (vortices) in the spine.

The spine may be compared to a bar magnet. The reason a bar of steel can be magnetized is that its molecules all have their own north-south polarity. In an ordinary bar of steel, the molecules are turned every which way, the magnetism of each canceling that of another. But if all those molecules can be influenced to turn in a north-south direction, the entire bar will become magnetized.

The vortices in the spine resemble those molecules in that, if their energy is not freed to flow in one direction, they obstruct the free manifestation of spiritual magnetism. In their case, being vortices, they obstruct the flow by drawing energy to a focus in themselves. Once their energy is released, it augments the upward flow of energy.

There are six centers in the spine—*chakras*, as they are called in the yoga tradition. In the physical body, these centers correspond to the neural plexuses that control the different organs of the body—heart, lungs, intestines, and so on.

The *vritti*s settle in the spine as an extension of the subconscious. Their location in the spine depends on the *chakra,* or spinal center, with which their vibrations are in harmony. The more spiritual a vortex, the higher the center around which it settles. The more materialistic a vortex, the lower the center. The energy of these vortices, when released to flow upward, combines to produce a mighty river of energy before which no obstacle can stand.

The job of releasing energy from billions of vortices would seem impossible, just as it would be to turn every molecule manually northward in a bar of steel. There are ways, however, of making the job relatively simple, just as in magnetizing a bar of steel. I'll go into the matter more deeply later on, but for now let me just say that a strong upward flow of energy in the spine dissolves those vortices automatically, just as a strong flow of water in a river dissolves the little eddies along its banks.

These *vritti*s form especially, as I said, around the spinal centers. All of them relate, however, directly or indirectly, to the heart center. Meditation on the heart, then, is particularly beneficial. There is one danger, however, in making the heart one's exclusive focus: The heart *chakra* is pivotal. Its energy can flow readily either upward or downward—upward toward enlightenment, or downward toward emotions that, even if spiritual at their inception, can sink gradually into emotionalism, then proceed to awaken sentiments that carry the mind back into delusion.

The heart's energy is already accustomed to flowing downward. Its impulse to do so must be kept constantly in check by discrimination and the will. For this reason, it is best to make one's main focus of concentration the point between the eyebrows. Bring the heart into the picture by consciously directing its energy upward toward that point.

At the same time, if one concentrates only in the center in the forehead, the seat of will, one may become ruthless. Such concentration must be supported by upward-flowing energy from the heart.

NAVI KRIYA

A yoga practice that has been adapted by Zen Buddhists* is to meditate in the area of the navel, corresponding to the *manipur chakra,* the lumbar center of the spine. When the energy of this center is directed up toward the brain, it generates great power of self-control. Lahiri Mahasaya taught concentration on this center at the start of the meditation period, so as to ground the mind and establish it in attitudes of firmness and resolution. To keep the mind centered wholly in this *chakra* could make a person *too* much grounded, even to the extent of making him solemn, not joyful. As a practice at the start of one's meditation period, however, this practice is excellent.

---

*The word *zen* has its roots in yoga tradition. It evolved out of the Sanskrit word *dhyan,* which means "meditation." *Dhyan* is the seventh stage of Patanjali's eight stages to enlightenment.

The technique is called *navi kriya*. It is practiced as follows:

1) Lower the chin slowly to the chest. Look upward throughout, toward the Spiritual Eye, and not downward at the navel. Breathe normally.

2) Mentally chant *AUM* (the word is pronounced "Om," and is often so written,* to rhyme with "home")

---

*I stopped writing it *Om* when I discovered that people in other countries, unfamiliar with the double sound of most vowels in English, were mispronouncing the vowel to sound like the "au" in "flaunt." Correct pronunciation of the word is important for its mantric power. The vowel has a double sound; in fact, it is composed of two vowels, a sound we get when we say the word "home."

There is a reason for the three sounds in this word: Each sound represents a distinct aspect of the Cosmic Vibration, out of which was produced all manifested creation. *A* (pronounced "aw" or "uh," not "ah") is the creative vibration, and is higher in pitch than the others. *U* (pronounced "oo" as in "moon") is the vibration that maintains the universe, preserving it in a state of equilibrium. Its pitch is lower. *M* is the vibration that dissolves creation back into the Spirit at the end of each cycle of cosmic manifestation. Its pitch is the lowest of the three: a deep, rumbling sound.

I have recorded this "*mantra* of all *mantras*" on CD and on audio-cassette. It is available from Clarity Sound and Light, 14618 Tyler-Foote Rd., Nevada City, CA 95959 (tel.: 800-424-1055).

The three aspects of the Cosmic Vibration have been personalized in Hindu mythology as Brahma, Vishnu, and Shiva—and woe to that rash *advaitin* (non-dualist) who tells the Hindu fundamentalist that these personages are only myths. In fact, so all-embracing is the beauty of *Sanatan Dharma*, (the Eternal Religion) that even the symbol is considered to be imbued with some of the power that it represents. A myth is real if it can bring cosmic truths to a focus.

The three aspects of *AUM* are coexistent, both in the universe and in the individual. Everything we do has a beginning, a middle, and an one hundred times, concentrating on the *manipur chakra,* the navel center.

3) Next, very slowly draw the chin upward until the head is tilted backward, though not so far that your neck is uncomfortable.

4) Chant *AUM* twenty-five times more.

5) Finally, return your head to its normal position and continue meditating.

Another practice that correlates interestingly with the yoga teachings is a Jewish tradition called *daven*ing, in which one sways one's body forward and backward while praying. This swaying motion bears a relationship to something the meditator actually experiences with the beginning of *kundalini* movement in the spine. *Daven*ing is not a technique for awakening the *kundalini* energy, but is rather something that may occur automatically with the early awareness of that awakening.

Thus, we see that the truths described here derive from universal realities, and have nothing to do with

---

end. As the sound of a car motor is highest when it first sets out in low gear, because the revolutions are higher, and lowest when the motor is shutting down, so the vibration of human creativity is different from that required to keep things on an even keel, and different again from that which is required for giving up anything and embracing change.

People whose lives run at an even flow—the Vishnu types—are often not comfortable around those who are highly creative—the higher-pitched Brahma types. And both tend to be uncomfortable around low-pitched Shiva types, who view everything as transient. In fact, however, we should strive to balance in ourselves all three aspects of human nature. Perfect equilibrium is the smoothest road to superconsciousness.

exclusive religious beliefs. Yoga is not a theory. It is an ongoing act of inner discovery.

****

MEDITATION EXERCISE

Concentrate at the point between the eyebrows. Visualize there a tunnel of golden light. Mentally enter that tunnel, and feel yourself surrounded by a glorious sense of happiness and freedom. As you move through the tunnel, feel yourself bathed by the light until all worldly thoughts disappear.

After soaring through the tunnel as long as you feel to so do, visualize before you a curtain of deep violet-blue light. Pass through that curtain into another tunnel of deep, violet-blue light. Feel the light surrounding you. Slowly, the tunnel walls disappear in blue light. Expand your consciousness into that light—into infinite freedom and bliss. Now there is no tunnel. There is only the all-encompassing blueness and bliss of infinity.

At last, visualize before you a silvery-white, five-pointed star of light. Mentally spread out your arms and legs, assuming with your body the shape of that star. Give yourself to it in body, mind, and soul as you surrender every thought, every feeling to absolute, Self-existing Bliss.

Bliss cascades gently over you, like a waterfall of mist, filling your heart with ineffable peace.

Chapter Ten

ENERGY: THE MISSED LINK

Energy is the link between mind and body—between consciousness and material creation.

When Spirit first manifested itself as cosmic creation, it projected itself outward into a state most closely resembling pure consciousness—in the form of thoughts and ideas. Vibrationless in itself, it set part of its undifferentiated being into vibratory movement. Thus was manifested the ideational, or causal, universe: causal, because from the level of thought forms were projected the vibrations that made grosser levels of manifestation possible.

Pure Consciousness, after creating the universe of ideational vibrations, worked through them to produce denser vibrations. Causative ideas became energy and light. Thus appeared the second stage of creation: the astral universe.

Pure Consciousness, finally, filtering, or stepping down, its vibrations as if through a transformer, descended through the stages of ideation and energy to manifest such dense vibrations that they appeared solid. Astral energy became matter. And thus was manifested the third and last stage of creation: the material universe.

Science, working backward from material appearances, has discovered that matter is not really substantial at all: It is a vibration of energy.

The astral universe is a projection of ideas—specific, not vague—that were formed in the causal universe. The material universe, similarly, is a projection of specific light and energy forms in the astral universe. In appearance, the astral universe is much like our own. Lacking matter's density, its vibrations are freer to separate themselves into individual, coherent spheres of consciousness and energy. Good and evil are not mingled in close proximity as they are on earth.

Even on earth, people tend somewhat to separate themselves into areas of compatible interests. Those whose natures are more refined tend to settle in neighborhoods with vibrations similar to their own. People of coarser natures gravitate toward other neighborhoods, compatible with themselves. I've been astonished to see how quickly—often, within hours—newcomers to a city will be drawn to their own vibrational milieu and meet people of whose very existence many long-term residents were completely unaware.

In the astral universe, whole planets have their own vibratory integrity. There are astral heavens, and astral hells. Differences among astral beings are understood to have nothing to do with skin color or other outward characteristics: They are entirely a matter of individual vibrations.

The material universe is no mere copy of the astral: It represents, rather, the necessary end product of cosmic creation. Without it, the subtler manifestations of energy, light, and thought would dissolve back again into Pure Consciousness. The material universe is, so to speak, the anchor of creation. It is like a stage play, written, rehearsed, and finally produced. Without final production, the energies of the actors, stagehands, director, and others would scatter and the play itself, lacking final commitment on the part of the cast, would, as it were, be reabsorbed into the playwright's personality. The existence of matter is necessary for holding it all together. Matter ensures that the cosmic play will have a long run to packed houses.

It is said that even the gods* consider experience of the material world a blessing, for it grounds the understanding and enables the soul thereby to evolve more quickly toward the highest wisdom. Truths often have to be brought "down to earth" before they can be fully understood. Teachers and writers, also, find that giving outward expression to their ideas helps to clarify them.

Creation, Paramhansa Yogananda wrote in *The Rubaiyat of Omar Khayyam Explained,* is like a building.[†]

---

*The gods correspond to the angels in Western terminology. Eastern religions contain many stories regarding the "gods" that are difficult for the modern mind to take literally. In fact, they are not meant to be taken literally. They are myths, replete with symbolism, intended to convey deep truths to unsophisticated audiences who, if their attention is to be held, require also to be entertained and amused. Much of humor the world over depends on a shared recognition of basic stereotypes.

[†]Nevada City, CA: Crystal Clarity, Publishers, 1994. I had the honor of editing this book.

The causal universe is like the architect's blueprint. The astral universe is like the energy necessary for constructing the building. And the material universe is like the building itself.

The outward movement of Pure Consciousness into vibration is more like a cosmic dance than a static tableau. It has momentum, the force of which brings clarity to its causative ideas, then passes on from there to activating the ideas as light and energy. Finally, it crystallizes that activating energy in material forms. The planning and energy that went into the creation of the physical universe, though invisible now behind a thick screen of illusion, are nonetheless present at the heart of everything.

Few people give a thought to the skill and energy that went into constructing a building. Fewer still ponder the nuances of meaning in the architect's vision. Similarly, people rarely pause to wonder how and for what purpose the universe came into existence.

A small child, knowing nothing of the process by which a building is constructed, might assume that buildings simply appear wherever people want them. In the same way, the children of Brooklyn used to believe that milk simply appeared on their doorsteps in bottles. At that time a cow was the most popular exhibit at the Bronx Zoo. To the children, it represented a miracle explained.

What Is a Miracle?

There are two common explanations for the Creation. One is, "There was this Big Bang, see, and it all just happened. Why? Well, it just happened, for no reason at all." The other explanation is that God simply "made" everything. *How?* Well, it was a miracle. Who needs an explanation for miracles?

Yet the mind isn't satisfied with either explanation. If the universe simply exploded into being, why is there not chaos? Why are there natural laws, such as gravitation, that maintain order among the galaxies and star systems? And why are the same laws operational everywhere? Doesn't it seem that the laws themselves predated the very existence of matter: that ideation preceded form?

As for miracles, what *is* a miracle? It is simply a phenomenon waiting to be explained. Television would have been a miracle to the people in medieval times. For that matter, the fact that it doesn't seem miraculous to us now isn't because most of us understand it. We accept it because it is commonplace. There is no such thing, really, as a bona fide miracle. There are only different workings of cosmic law.

If the mysteries of creation seem irrelevant to our present human needs, my purpose in discussing them is not abstract, but practical and immediate. Even the discoveries astronomers have made regarding distant stars and galaxies have had many practical consequences for mankind.

Science will never be able to trace the genesis of the universe to its ultimate source, for it is obliged by its own disciplines to approach reality from its periphery, not from its center. Creation, on the other hand, is like a living tree: It is a radiation outward from its center in

Pure Consciousness. The mysteries of cosmic creation can be solved only by people who, in deep meditation, succeed in penetrating to the core of their own being—which, they find, is the center of Being everywhere.

Creation, as the great masters explain it, puts into perspective certain vitally important aspects of our own lives. Their explanation clarifies how we can heal ourselves and others; how we can be more creative; how we can attract inspiration at will, and generate the magnetism by which to draw success to ourselves. Above all, it explains how we can develop spiritually without waiting passively for a benign Providence to make it all happen for us.

The "missing link" between mind and body, between an idea and its fulfillment, and between aspiration and success is in every case the same thing: energy.

ENERGY AND WILL

Try a simple experiment: Raise your right arm. See? All you need do is mentally tell it to rise, and it rises.

Now then, try something else. Tell your arm to rise, but don't send any energy to make it do so. What happens? It hasn't moved, has it?

Try something else: Send energy to the arm, but don't tell the arm to rise. Again, you see? No movement.

We all know that the mind acts upon the body. Medical science accepts that it can sometimes heal the body, too. Happiness has been known to cure. Depression has been known to make people ill.

What is not generally known is the *way* the mind acts on the body. Moving a limb is so commonplace an act that people take it for granted. What makes it obey our commands? We don't even bother to ask.

Yet nothing purposeful occurs on its own. There is a missing link here. Why can I tell my arm to rise, and expect it to obey, whereas if I tell a cup on my kitchen table to rise, it won't? It isn't only that my nervous system connects the brain to the arm. It's that I can send *energy* through the nerves to the arm with my command that it rise.

The mind cannot act directly upon the body. It must act through the medium of energy. The will first acts upon the energy. The energy then acts upon the body. This process is basically like the process of cosmic creation itself. It is the way our bodies were made: Cosmic thought, through cosmic energy, and finally through the agency of our individual karma, willed the creation of the body.

The mind continues to control the body through the medium of energy. Automatic functions, such as digestion and breathing, are carried on for the most part without our conscious involvement, but under the guidance of the subconscious mind.

When we become ill, the cause of our illness lies primarily in a disruption of the energy-flow from the mind. The metaphysical cause of disease, Paramhansa Yogananda stated, is a conflict between the upward and downward movements of energy in the spine: the one, toward affirmation; the other, toward negation. The greater this conflict, the more it weakens the flow of energy in the body, and projects subtle vibrations of disturbance.

As the flow of energy depends on the mind, so the *strength* of that flow depends on our mental strength. The elimination of the inner conflict Yogananda described results in a greatly strengthened will, and therefore in a greatly increased flow of energy. For the will is like a rheostat: It can diminish the energy-flow by our unwillingness or disinterest, or increase that flow immeasurably by our willingness and enthusiasm.

Paramhansa Yogananda put it axiomatically: *The greater the will, the greater the flow of energy.* You can test the truth of this statement very easily. Simply tense your biceps. The more you *will* energy to the biceps, the harder it will tense. The same principle acts in reverse, also: The more you withdraw your will from the muscle, telling it to relax, the deeper will be the relaxation.

The analogy of a rheostat is helpful for another reason also. A rheostat reduces the lighting in a room by obstructing the flow of electricity; it doesn't increase that flow by augmenting the natural voltage in the line. Many people make the mistake of trying to increase their will power by straining the mind, as though it were a muscle. Their effort is evident in their furrowed foreheads and fiercely knitted eyebrows. Strain is counterproductive. You may find it helpful to emphasize *willingness,* rather than exerting your will power grimly. For the will, to be maximally effective, must be relaxed. Simply focus your mind with complete concentration on anything you want to accomplish. Paramhansa Yogananda defined will power as "desire plus energy directed toward fulfillment."

You can energize your body at will. For its energy doesn't depend on food, air, and sunlight alone. We live surrounded by an ocean of cosmic energy, and draw on it to a greater or lesser extent all the time, depending on our will power, or willingness, and on the clarity of our awareness. This energy enters our bodies just as it did in the creation of the body, through the medulla oblongata. For this reason, too, you will find it helpful during meditation to deepen your awareness of the medulla.

The Importance of Energy

Energy is the cornerstone of the yoga teachings. Many meditation teachings insist that to rise above body-consciousness one should ignore the body altogether. In so doing they demonstrate philosophical purity, but fall short of rational clarity. The fact is, we cannot afford to ignore the body. We must eat to stay alive. We must breathe, sleep, and in many ways respond to the body's needs. Even if our goal in life is to meditate, we may as well accept that our bodies are real to us in our present state of existence. They can be ignored only at our peril.

An airplane pilot, before flying, may be mentally already soaring in the heavens, but he knows that to fly safely the essential parts of his plane must be checked carefully to make sure they are functional.

Vagueness in meditation produces vague results. Similarly, vagueness in our interaction with the body produces only vague success in our attempts to rise above body-consciousness. Better than ignoring the body is to understand how body-consciousness obstructs meditation, and then to remove the actual cause of that obstruction.

Energy is the link, usually missed, between body and mind. For lack of awareness of the energy, many meditators never get off the ground, metaphorically speaking. That is why Sri Krishna in the *Bhagavad Gita*, addressing this particular controversy, says, "O Arjuna, be thou a yogi!"

Energy, the communicating link between body and mind, also ties the mind down to the body if we simply ignore its existence. Imagine a balloon secured to the ground by guy lines. The balloonist, to rise in the air, must release the guy lines.

In meditation, trying to rise while ignoring the energy-link between mind and body is like increasing the quantity of helium in a balloon in the hope of eventually bursting the guy lines. Why not do both? Increase your rising devotion, of course, but at the same time take practical steps to withdraw the energy from the senses.

Meditators do occasionally achieve success in meditation without taking practical steps to withdraw their energy from body-consciousness, but it is because they have inadvertently brought the energy under control by their devotional fervor. Such results, for lack of practical awareness of the process involved, are uncertain. The very process of bursting the guy lines of energy by strengthening the upward pull upon them damages the body. Why not take a little extra trouble? Simply untie the ropes!

Let me take another example: If a garden hose is bent double, the hose may be damaged if the flow of water is increased. We see in the lives of many saints that they underwent great physical suffering as they developed spiritually. So common is this occurrence that physical suffering has been made almost a demonstration of sainthood! It needn't be so. Much of this suffering—not all of it, for suffering is also necessary to the development of wisdom—would have been avoided had they been more cognizant of the way the energy flows in the body.

THE FOURTH STAGE: *PRANAYAMA*

The fourth stage of meditation is called *Pranayama* in Sanskrit. *Pranayama* means "control of the body's energy." This stage is important because, to attain soul-freedom, the energy must be calmed, then directed inward from the senses to the brain.

Two things are important for bringing the energy under control: awareness, and will power. The greater the will, the greater the flow of that energy. And the greater the awareness of that energy, the easier it will be for us to redirect it toward the Spiritual Eye.

Paramhansa Yogananda created a unique system, which he called "energization exercises," to help people in attaining this energy-control. His system helps to direct energy to the body and, afterward, to withdraw it again from the body in meditation. These exercises give awareness of the energy, and, by means of that awareness, the ability to manipulate its flow in the body at will.

By practicing these exercises daily, you'll develop exceptional ability to heal your body, and even—a subject I'll discuss in the next chapter—to achieve success in your outward undertakings. You'll find it possible to attract desired opportunities, and to draw inspiration at will.

I've experienced the effectiveness of these exercises many times, in little ways and in great. Here is one example—a little one.

Five months ago, I underwent open heart surgery to replace a faulty valve. The day before surgery, as I was being prepared for the operation, I addressed an urgent task: the editing of the foreword to a new book of mine, which was due to go to the printer immediately. The day following surgery, my mind still wanting to accept the cloudiness caused by the general anaesthesia, I brushed aside the fog and completed the task. It would have been much more difficult for me to cut through the mental mist had I not known and practiced these principles for many years.

The energization exercises, to be learned effectively, require demonstration. If you'd like to learn them (the entire set requires about ten to twelve minutes to complete), I suggest you visit or write to The Expanding Light.* This is a retreat facility of Ananda Village, a community I founded in 1968 for people who want to practice and live according to these principles.

---

*14618 Tyler-Foote Rd., Nevada City, CA 95959 (telephone: 800-346-5350 or 530-478-7518).

For now, let me suggest you practice just one exercise from this system:

Stand upright. Inhale slowly, gradually tensing the whole body (low, medium, high) to the point where it vibrates. Gaze upward at the point between the eyebrows, and with concentration feel the energy flowing into the body through the medulla oblongata. Hold the tension for a few moments, and consciously fill the whole body with energy. Then exhale and slowly relax (medium, low, completely), *feeling* the energy as it withdraws from the body parts. Always tense with will, then relax and *feel*.

Anytime you feel a need to energize, or to heal, an individual body part, tense that part with will power, sending energy to it from the medulla; then relax it, as I've described doing with the whole body, and feel the energy withdraw.

While tensing, be aware of the body *inwardly*, not outwardly. Concentrate in the center of any part you are tensing. Once you become inwardly aware of that tension, you will gradually become aware of the energy creating it. The more aware you are of the energy, the greater will be your control over it.

****

MEDITATION EXERCISE

I suggested earlier that you begin your meditation by tensing and relaxing the body two or three times. Let me now suggest that you bring greater will power and deeper awareness to this practice.

The best way to relax the body in meditation is consciously to withdraw the energy from it. *Pranayama* techniques in yoga books usually focus on breathing exercises. *Prana* is also, in fact, the Sanskrit word for "breath"; there exists a close connection between the breath and the energy, or life-force. Those breathing exercises are particularly useful in helping to raise the energy in the spine.

For now, try again the exercise I recommended earlier: Inhale, gradually tensing the whole body until it vibrates. Be fully aware of the energy behind that tension and vibration. Then exhale forcibly and relax, releasing the energy from the muscles. With relaxation, feel the energy withdrawing from the body. Repeat this exercise two or three times. Then take several deep, slow breaths, as I've suggested before: Inhale counting to 12, hold counting to 12, exhale counting to 12. Then, with deep relaxation, draw the energy up the spine by concentration at the point between the eyebrows.

Meditate on space, and on the feeling of freedom from body-awareness. Direct your energy with joyful will power and devotional fervor through the Spiritual Eye in the forehead, out into Infinity.

Chapter Eleven

ENERGY: THE KEY TO SUCCESS AND WELL-BEING

"Your religion is tested in the cold light of day." So said a great woman saint. Every step inward on the spiritual path must be secured by some outward reassurance that we are on the right track. We cannot, for example, be truly growing in divine love if we are uncharitable toward others. We cannot honestly claim to be receiving intuitive inner guidance if in our outer lives we generate confusion. And if we find we can't cope with the practical demands of life, we can't very well make daily meditation the excuse for our woolly-mindedness.

It is not a rule that every gain in the material world must indicate a gain in the spiritual. Nor is it a rule that material losses indicate comparable spiritual losses. Illness, for example, may occur even among people who are highly advanced. The intricacies of karma, brought over from countless incarnations, make it impossible to establish absolute rules. The *vrittis* (vortices of energy) in the spine are no simple matter to dissolve. We can't neutralize them by meditation alone until we attain high spiritual advancement. It is divine grace, ultimately, that rescues us, entering our temples when we have swept and cleaned them and done our part to make them holy places. Meanwhile, the important thing is to go to God, and not worry about all those kinks, *vrittis*, and obstacles you have churning about within you, blocking your progress toward absolute freedom.

Jesus Christ gave the world a wonderful statement: "Seek ye first the kingdom of God, and His righteousness, and all these things shall be added unto you." Make it your priority to discharge your highest duty, to find God, and God will do the rest.

The modern way to "perfection" is very different. It is to try to work out our psychological kinks through counseling sessions. This is good up to a point, certainly, provided the counselor is wise, and provided that all one wants to address are the most pressing and immediate issues. But if our goal is "the kingdom of God," remember that those kinks may well number in the billions, including the myriads of *vrittis* spinning away in the subconscious. To seek perfection through a purely psychological approach is like trying to submerge a shirt in water when you're washing it by hand. A bubble forms, and you push the shirt down at that point only to see the bubble move off to another part of the shirt.

Go straight to God. He will take care of the rest. Work on those kinks which particularly trouble you, but above all offer them to God. It is from the higher part of our consciousness that true understanding comes. By working on ourselves from the superconscious level, we find that it becomes actually a blessing to discover faults in ourselves. Each one gives us the joyful opportunity to offer something more to God. He can purify us, as no amount of psychological counseling and self-analysis ever will.

Above all, offer your ego to God. It is His power that you use, or misuse, in any case. No other power exists in the universe. But if you can bring yourself to feel that He, and not your ego, is the doer of everything accomplished through you, it will be increasingly difficult for you to misuse that power, since abuse of it springs from ego-consciousness.

Your job is to perfect yourself by divine power, not by ego power. Self-effort is essential. Jesus said so, too, in his statement, "Be ye therefore perfect, even as your Father which is in heaven is perfect" (Matthew 5:48).

Go straight to God. Become, in the Sanskrit terminology, a *jivanmukta*, "freed while living." In that state, God will give you the power to sweep away all lingering obstacles, or will Himself remove them for you. In that state, past karma can be worked out in visions or in other ways. If you open wide the doors of your inner temple, it will be easier to sweep the dust out. The breeze of divine grace will do most of the sweeping for you.

The fact that inner progress must have objective verification can easily be mistaken to mean that we must concentrate more on the verification than on our inner progress. I once knew a lady who was determined to attain spiritual liberation by first becoming a millionaire. To her way of thinking, the inability to manifest great wealth demonstrated a spiritual weakness, and was a fault that needed to be overcome on the material plane. Such a practice is like changing the number on the bathroom scales from zero to minus ten to persuade oneself that one has lost ten pounds. Outer demonstrations are a means of testing inner gains, but are not the way to achieve those gains.

I've known people also who believed that good health was a proof of spirituality, whereas bad health demonstrated the opposite. To become "spiritual," they undertook long fasts, and in other ways devoted so much time to perfecting their physical bodies that they had little time left over for an inner life. Ironically, such people often become actually weaker than others who are cheerfully devoted to a diet of "meat and potatoes." It isn't their diet that weakens them: It is their constant preoccupation with diet, and with their bodies, to the extent that they lose touch with the sustaining energy *within* their bodies.

The intricacies of karma are such that no amount of outer effort will ever unravel them. They are like the mythical Gordian knot, impossible to untie because, even if one manages to get one strand released, in that very act another one gets tightened.

Sir Walter Scott's quote is helpful in this regard, if we add to it just one word: "Oh, what a tangled web we weave when first we practice to deceive" *ourselves*. We deceive ourselves every time we seek fulfillment in the world of the senses. Vast numbers of *vritti*s in the subconscious work against one another. The only way to work them out, finally and forever, is to cut the Gordian knot as Alexander the Great did. In the present case, the cut must be made by the "sword" of calmness and discrimination, born of meditation.

THE RIGHT USE OF PRAYER

What is the right attitude for one who is bent on achieving liberation from ego? My own recommendation is this: Be stern with yourself on the big issues, but not too heavy on the smaller ones. Your spiritual life should be a joy. Don't agonize, for instance, over whether it is wrong to pray for snow, if you want to go skiing. At the same time, remember this: Many thin strands make a rope. Don't pray too often even for little things for yourself.

My own rule—to me it seems a good one, though I don't necessarily recommend it to anyone—is this: I wouldn't dream of praying that my life be spared, but I wouldn't at all mind praying for a box of chocolates if I wanted some. Incidentally, when I say *pray,* I don't mean *supplicate.* I mean simply to share my thoughts and wishes with God. What I also do is ask God, "Is it all right to pray for this blessing?" If, in my heart, I receive a negative response to that question, I obey that response.

There is another rule I follow, more important to me than any other: I will pray if the welfare of others is concerned, but generally speaking I won't pray for my own welfare.

Here are a couple of stories that may be worth relating:

One Sunday morning, some twenty-five years ago, I was to give the service at our temple at Ananda Village.

Suddenly I had a kidney stone attack. "Attack" is the right word: My whole body trembled from the pain like a leaf in a high wind. At no other time have I suffered anything remotely like it. Someone insisted that I be taken to the local hospital, but the mere thought of that forty-five-minute drive on winding mountain roads was too much for me even to contemplate. Unable to speak, I could only ignore the well-meant advice. But I still wouldn't pray for myself. All I prayed was "This body is Yours. Do with it what You want."

After more than an hour, I glanced at my watch and saw that the service was scheduled to begin in fifteen minutes. I'd been in extreme pain all that time. Now I prayed, "If You don't want me to disappoint all those people, make this body well."

The results were amazing. Within five seconds, as though someone had waved a healing wand over my body, the pain vanished completely. As excruciating as the pain had been earlier, it was now replaced by a divine joy equally intense, so much so that this joy, too, rendered me almost speechless! Somehow I managed to get through the service, but few of the people present realized that the tears which made speech difficult for me were tears of joy, not of pain.

On the other hand, I had a hip replacement operation some years ago. The surgeon told me he'd never before seen such a bad case. He'd had to replace two inches of bone, worn away over years from stress induced by walking. "I don't know how you managed it," he told me. In fact, walking had not been easy. My friends exclaimed later, "We had no idea you were in so much pain!" But—well, why bore people with little things? Why even bother God?

There was another time, however, years earlier, when I saw no need for such sternness. In the early 1950s, my parents were living in France. Dad was the chief geologist for Esso in Europe. The thought came to me to include in a letter to them a special request. As a schoolboy in Switzerland in the 1930s, I'd enjoyed Swiss chocolate. As far as I knew at that time, Swiss chocolate wasn't available in America. Now it occurred to me that, since my parents lived relatively close to Switzerland, perhaps they would be able to send me some.

The desire was trivial, so much so that I kept forgetting to mention it in my letters. But when my birthday drew near, the thought suddenly came to me, "What a pity!" I shared that thought with God, to whom I pray as my Divine Mother. "Too bad, Divine Mother! It would have been nice to have those chocolates for my birthday." I then dismissed the thought.

The day before my birthday, almost a week later, I received a box of Swiss chocolates from a friend in Hollywood who didn't know it was my birthday, and knew nothing of my fondness for them. Accompanying the box was a letter, which read, "I was passing a store window today when I saw this box of Swiss chocolates. Suddenly I thought of you, and felt a desire to send them." To me, the gift was sweeter than if my life had been threatened, and miraculously saved. The desire itself was, as I said, trivial; I passed out most of the chocolates to my friends. But the sweetness in the thought that the Divine Mother would express love for me in such a little matter has remained with me these more than forty years.

To make a big philosophical issue in such a case, by refusing to ask God for help, would have been, it seems to me, excessively severe for a path of which the goal is eternal joy. Moreover, I didn't actually ask Divine Mother for help. All I did was share with Her my petty disappointment. Was that why She responded so promptly?

I have asked for God's help many times in my service to Him (or, as I put it, to Her). Many people have called the responses to those prayers miraculous.

In every case, what made these "graces" possible was the attraction of energy, by will power, from the surrounding universe. Even my walking, when X-rays showed me incapable of doing so, was due to "grace" of a kind. For faith itself must be dynamic, not passive. By offering it to God, we focus it better. But in any case, it is the divine energy we use, whether we ask for it specifically or direct the energy ourselves. Half-hearted prayer brings at best a half-hearted response. Effective prayer demands that we offer it up with strong will power, with complete confidence in the rightness of the outcome, and with an awareness of the energy required for results.

To put this principle to most effective use, try sending energy out through the Spiritual Eye, the seat of will. You will actually feel that energy as a force flowing out through your forehead.

Another technique is to draw energy to your palms by rubbing them together briskly, thirty to sixty times. Then raise the hands high above the head, palms forward, and send the energy that you feel tingling in the hands to those for whom you are praying. Feeling the energy entering through the medulla and out through the palms, chant *AUM* three to twelve times, holding each tone as long as you can do so comfortably.

Remember, your mind is part of the Infinite Mind. The more you unite your awareness to the divine consciousness, the more effective your power will be. You alone can't do it all.

The power of the will backed by Cosmic Will may be compared to a violin string backed by the violin's sounding board. If the string is stretched between two points in space and the bow is then drawn across it, the sound produced will be very thin. But when the string is positioned on a violin, that same bow stroke can fill a concert hall with sound.

Often, far more good is accomplished for others, and even for ourselves, when we ask for nothing, but only offer ourselves up to superconsciousness to do with us what it wills.

I mentioned in the last chapter the operation I had on my heart five months ago. The reason for the operation was that my heart had enlarged so much that any further enlargement would have sent it into a permanent decline. Moreover, I had been in atrial fibrillation; the irregularity of my heartbeat had been so extreme that I remarked to someone, "No composer could write music to *this* beat!" For several weeks before the operation I had a heartbeat of about 160. Worse still, tests showed that the heart sometimes slowed down briefly at night to 30 beats a minute. Because a third of that blood was pumping backward anyway, there was a possibility that I might die of heart failure in my sleep. My heart output was less than 30 percent of normal. In short, I was a cardiac cripple.

When my cardiologist told me I needed an operation, I asked him, "Is there any chance my heart might shrink again after the operation?"

"No chance of that," he replied. "But at least you'll be pumping all your blood in the right direction. This means the heart won't enlarge any further, and won't go into that decline I'm worried about."

I prayed silently, "Divine Mother, this is Your body. Do with it what You want." I didn't pray for help. For years I'd prayed, however, to be able to serve as an instrument for bringing others to the spiritual path. It was to this lifelong prayer that the Divine Mother responded. Many other people, also, were praying for my safe recovery; unquestionably, their prayers helped greatly with the healing process.

After the operation, the surgeon told me, "We've done what we can, but I'm afraid there's no chance you'll ever come out of atrial fibrillation."

The following day I was out of it! The cardiologist addressed me later that day, his face a study in amazement. "I have to tell you this," he said. "The chances of your coming out of atrial fibrillation were *zero*."

A month later, an X-ray of my chest showed that my heart had shrunk back to normal size: a reduction of 50 percent.

Three months later, an echocardiogram showed the heart pumping at the high end of normal: 70 percent. A normal heart empties 60 to 70 percent of its chamber. The heart of a young athlete in good physical condition may empty as much as 75 percent. Mine, to repeat, had been less than 30 percent.

I didn't ask for any of this, though certainly I'm grateful for the outcome, since it means I can now put more energy into serving God than I've been able to do for many years.

The important thing, here, is to realize that: 1) the human mind is part of an infinitely greater consciousness; 2) the more one offers one's life up in service to God, the greater one's power to accomplish whatever one sets oneself to do; 3) this self-offering must be dynamic, not static, and must summon up all one's will power and enthusiasm; and 4) an unspecific prayer will often have greater results than praying for something definite. God knows our true needs better than we do.

It is true that superconsciousness is demonstrated outwardly by a person's mastery over matter. It is also true that such demonstrations are sometimes helpful, if only to convince ourselves that we have not, in meditation, been "practicing self-deceit." Healing ourselves of an illness can be a demonstration of spiritual power. It is not wrong for someone who is still aware of himself as the ego to pray for personal healing. Take care only that it not cause you to give undue importance to the ego.

If I won't pray for myself, it is to avoid ego-involvement. I consider it much more freeing in any case to offer the big tests up to God and let Him (Her) decide the outcome.

You don't have to be forever "demonstrating" your meditative achievements. Not only would the attempt distract you from your meditative efforts: It might also cost you a few friendships! For who wants to be around people who are forever "proving" things? Of course— inevitably so—you *will* use these principles of will power and energy in your own life. And so you should.

Meditation will make your whole outlook on life dynamic, forceful, energetic, and enthusiastic. Success and well-being will come to you as a matter of course. You will attract them by your developing magnetism.

Spiritual attainment is not for weaklings. It is for people of dynamic will power and energy. Never imagine that to be spiritual is to be "meek and mild" in the milquetoast sense. Jesus, whom many Christians emulate for his meekness as they imagine it to have been, was in no way a bird with a broken wing: He was a spiritual dynamo! The fact that meekness is mentioned in the Beatitudes in connection with an extraordinary blessing ("Blessed are the meek, for they shall inherit the earth") makes it clear that Jesus was not saying, "Blessed are the milksops." What it takes to inherit the earth is to live in harmony with it, not to smile in weak apology for everything that happens, or doesn't happen, as though one were forever personally to blame.

"Blessed are the harmonious." That is what Jesus meant. Harmonious toward others and toward the world: That is what God, through the teachings of all the great masters, asks us to be.

In the next chapter I shall discuss further the subject of magnetism, by which we can attract all good.

Meanwhile, let me propose a meditation exercise to deepen your attunement to the Cosmic Will.

****

MEDITATION EXERCISE

Imagine yourself on a surfboard. Wait a little for the wave you want. Allow lesser waves to pass under you. (Opportunity must be embraced with your whole will, and not accepted with the thought that you may just as well ride one wave as another.)

When the right wave comes along, stand on your surfboard with calm, joyful confidence and enthusiasm. Realize that you are being carried along by the wave, not by your own power. Your task, now, is to cooperate with the wave. But remember, cooperation requires active participation, not passive acquiescence.

Don't think about the beach toward which the wave is rushing. Don't worry about how far you will rise. Twist, turn, dip, and lift your board joyfully.

At a certain point, enter the great curl of the wave as it crashes down upon itself.

Affirm all the while, "I am one with the wave, one with its sweeping movement, one with the entire ocean!"

Chapter Twelve

MAGNETISM

There are many fascinating correlations between spirituality and the physical sciences. Newton's third law of motion ("For every action there is an equal and opposite reaction") has its counterpart in the spiritual law of karma, according to which every deed attracts to the doer a just and compensating result. The force of gravity has its counterpart in the power of love. Magnetism, too, is a spiritual as well as a mundane principle.

Electricity flowing through an electric wire generates a magnetic field. The stronger the electric flow, the broader and stronger the field.

Energy flowing through the nerves of the body also produces a kind of electromagnetic field. This field is much subtler than any with which science is familiar, but it has much greater power to affect people and events.

The will determines the strength of the energy-flow ("the greater the will, the greater the flow of energy"). If the will power is strong, the body will be filled with energy. As a consequence, the body's magnetic field will be extensive and powerful. But in this context there is another important consideration: the *quality* of that energy, and therefore of that magnetism.

For there are many different states of consciousness, and therefore many different kinds of subtle energy. If our consciousness is strongly positive, our magnetism will be positive also, and will attract good things to us. It will, in addition, create a "buffer zone" around us, protecting us from harm; like an umbrella in the rain, it will fend off much of the suffering we might otherwise attract by negative karmic vortices (*vrittis*) of energy in the spine. Sri Krishna referred to this protection in the *Bhagavad Gita:* "Even a little practice of this spiritual discipline will free you from dire fears and colossal sufferings."

The laws of magnetism can work in extraordinary ways. I was told a story about Theos Bernard by a friend of his. Bernard was an American who went to Tibet some sixty years ago and there studied certain esoteric teachings, including laws that govern spiritual magnetism. Thinking to instruct the Los Angeles police force in non-violent methods of self-defense, he went and offered to teach them something of what he knew.

The police officers laughed at him. Finally, exasperated, he challenged them: "All right, come to me one at a time and take a swing at me." There were fifteen men in the room. This was an invitation they could accept happily. One by one they stepped up, drew back and let fly with a "haymaker." Each in turn passed out before his fist even touched Bernard, who calmly walked out of the room, leaving fifteen insensate bodies on the floor behind him.

Paramhansa Yogananda was once meditating in his upstairs bedroom when, in vision, he saw a burly young man, extremely hostile to the spiritual teachings, on his way up the stairs to give him a beating. The young man's intention was to broadcast to the world his boast that spirituality was no match for physical force.

The master prayed for guidance. He didn't want to hurt the young man. At the same time, he asked if God wanted this lie spread about the spiritual teachings he'd been sent to disseminate in the West. The answer he got was to defend himself without physical violence.

As the youth appeared in the doorway, Yogananda said, "I know why you've come."

"Go on, prophet!" sneered the young man. "I'm going to beat you up!"

"I want you to know," the master replied, "that I could easily beat you, physically. I'm much stronger than you know. But God doesn't want me to use physical force. Nevertheless, I warn you: Don't cross that threshold."

"Go on, prophet!" the youth sneered again. Boldly he crossed the threshold. A moment later he fell screaming to the floor. "I'm on fire!" he cried. "I'm on fire!" Leaping to his feet, he raced down the stairs and out of the building. Yogananda hastily descended the stairs, and found the man rolling about on the lawn in front of the building still crying, "I'm on fire!" Touching him, the master banished the pain instantly. "Don't touch me!" cried the man, panic-stricken. He wouldn't reenter the building, but got his sister, who lived there, to gather his things. Within the hour he left the property, and never returned.

So as not to leave the reader thinking that human magnetism is only a kind of spiritual weapon, I'll tell one more story about Yogananda.

One evening on a street corner, three holdup men approached him and demanded his money. Giving them all he had, he told them, "I'm happy to give you what is in my wallet. But I have another treasure that you'll never be able to take from me, unless I give it to you freely."

"What's the matter with this guy?" they demanded of one another. "Is he crazy?"

The master then looked at them with the magnetic power of divine love. The three of them began to tremble. "We can't take your money!" they cried. "What have you done to us?" Terrified of this unexpected experience, they ran away into the night.

One simple principle for developing positive magnetism is to keep your will positive and harmonious. It will help you to attune yourself to superconsciousness.

THE THREE "BANDS": *GUNAS*

As white light is composed of the full spectrum of the rainbow, so, too, energy is not a single force, but is composed of a broad spectrum. As there are rays of light far subtler than anything visible to the physical eyes, so, too, energy contains a broad range of vibrations, far subtler than anything measurable by physical instruments. Comparable to the three levels of creation—ideational, astral, and material—there are three main bands in the spectrum of vibration, and also therefore in the spectrum of energy.

The first of these bands contains vibrations that are spiritually uplifting—light, as opposed to heavy. The second is activating, or energizing; in human beings, it may be described as ego-activating. The third is dense; we may designate it as heavy.

These three bands (*gunas*, they are called in Sanskrit) are present in varying degrees throughout creation. Without them, nothing could have been brought into manifestation.

The three *gunas* may be compared, in a sense, to the molecules in a bar magnet, each of which has a north-south polarity, no more so at the north end of the bar of steel than at the south. Magnetism results from a directional flow of energy. The second *guna* in this analogy is the flow of energy itself, passing between the two poles.

In every part of creation, similarly, there is an energy-flow between two polar opposites, the flow itself being the second *guna* (quality, or attribute). In the cosmic scheme of things, duality is seen in the two poles, the "south" pole representing the material universe, and the "north" pole representing the ideational. The energy flowing between the two represents the astral universe. This "middle ground" of energy represents both a north-ward and a southward flow. The opposition that exists, thereby, in the world of energy results in the vibrational gradations of heavens and hells.

In sentient beings, the presence of these three *gunas* manifests in similar ways: in *tamo guna* (the darkening, heavy quality) as a tendency toward dullness and stupidity; in *rajo guna* (the activating quality) as restlessness, indecision, and vacillation born of the constant conflict between the two "poles"; and in *sattwa guna* (the lightest quality) as a calm inner pull toward purity and an expansive spirit.

Every human being manifests these three qualities to varying degrees, depending on the vibrations of his consciousness and energy. If his flow of energy is entirely upward, it gains in refinement until at last he passes beyond the three *guna*s into the pure, vibrationless Spirit. If the flow is downward, his understanding becomes increasingly dull until there is little, apart from his human form, to distinguish him from the lower animals. And if he lives, as most people do, in a state of indecision and inner conflict between these two directional flows, he remains tossing back and forth, forever agitated and restless.

The great majority of human beings fall into this third category. They may feel themselves drawn more toward one "pole" or another, but their inner conflict remains unresolved. People of unrefined, or heavy, consciousness seldom have strong enough magnetism to project their spiritual heaviness onto others. It is people in the ego-active category who have the greatest potential for lowering the magnetism of others. Possessing greater energy, they may also be magnetic even though their flow of energy is downward.

Avoid like the plague anyone whose magnetism has the power to pull you down. Such a person is worse for you than any disease. For physical disease affects only the body, but spiritual disease can devastate you spiritually.

People who are calm, non-violent, self-controlled, and truthful emanate an uplifting magnetism. Their mere presence is healing and uplifting to others. That is why the Indian scriptures say, "Even a moment in the presence of a saint will be your boat over the ocean of delusion."

THE LAW OF MAGNETISM

We affect others by our magnetism. They in return, by their magnetism, affect us. It is vitally important to understand the principles of magnetism, how they can be used for our own and others' benefit, how to benefit from others' magnetism, and how to protect ourselves against harmful magnetism in others.

Sat-sanga (good company) is almost as important on the path as meditation itself. Mix more with spiritually minded people. Tune in *consciously* to their vibrations. As you draw from others, so give love and appreciation in return. By thus closing the energy circuit, you will help bring about a mutual increase of magnetism. (To draw on others like a sponge is to drain their energy without in any way increasing your own. For your energy increases only if you raise your vibrations, never if you lower them.)

A negative human magnet can actually sap the power of a positive magnet, if the latter is inattentive, and especially if the negative magnetism is the stronger. On the other hand, if the positive magnet is the stronger it won't be deeply affected, especially if it is attentive and consciously maintains a magnetic shield. If it is much stronger, it may actually succeed in converting the negative flow in the other person to a positive one. Here is an earnest suggestion, however: Don't, in the name of loving all, take chances with your own magnetism.

I had an interesting experience in Jerusalem, twelve years ago, that illustrates this principle for me. I took a quick photograph of an Arab woman seated on the street, selling vegetables. My thought was simply to get an interesting photograph. The woman, however, perhaps taking me for a Jew, or perhaps responding to some religious stricture against being photographed, reacted with extreme anger. Shouting some imprecation, she hurled some small object at me—a nut, or a small vegetable: whatever it was, she missed me. Her hatred, however, remained with me. It took me several hours to shake off the disturbing impression it made on me.

Had I been able to offer her something, perhaps I would not have been so adversely affected. As it was, I prayed for her. Divine love is our greatest protection.

You will grow faster spiritually if you try to serve others. Don't serve them, however, beyond a realistic appraisal of your own magnetic strength.

Sat-sanga is important for another reason also: When spiritually inclined people get together, especially for meditation, they increase the magnetism of everyone involved. Yogananda called this phenomenon "the law of invisible vibratory exchange."

There are ways of protecting yourself from negative magnetism, and ways also of developing positive magnetism. Beware, however, of using spiritual power for ego-gratification. I'm sure it is just as well the Los Angeles police rejected Theos Bernard's offer to teach them his techniques of magnetic self-defense. Yes, there are words of power (*mantras*, they are called) by which you can affect objective reality. You can also, by concentrating at the point between the eyebrows and rotating the will powerfully around the thought of self, learn to send powerful thoughts from your own spiritual center to that center in others whom you want to affect. But beware of hurting anyone. In such cases there is a boomerang effect. The action must be for their welfare, and must proceed from higher consciousness. Beware, above all, of reawakening the delusion in your own subconscious that an outward direction of energy is desirable.

If you are faced with negative influences, and can't avoid them, here are a few helpful suggestions for how to cope with them:

1) If those influences come to you unsolicited, remember: They may have been sent to help you grow stronger in yourself. A hothouse plant grows larger and more luxuriant than its cousins out of doors, exposed as they are to wind, rain, and cold, but it has less stamina. What I am saying about magnetism, then, mustn't make you cowardly. Take it only as a reminder to be prudent.

2) If you know you are going to be exposed to *tamasic* vibrations, take the time to meditate beforehand. Then harmonize the vibrations of your heart. Next, *consciously* emanate peaceful vibrations outward from your heart center to your environment. For human energy

has two modes of expression; one of them is giving, the other, receiving or absorbing. If you can consciously enter the giving mode, you will find yourself much less affected by outside influences, whether good or bad. (For this reason it is wise also, as much as possible, to sleep and eat in a harmonious environment. For at such times, your energy is in the absorbing, or receiving, mode.)

3) Mentally chant, according to the sincere call of your heart: for example, "I am Thine. Be Thou mine," or, less personally, "I am light. I am love. I am a fountain of unending peace!"

4) Send the heart's energy upward to the point between the eyebrows. Feel yourself surrounded and embraced by the divine light.

5) In the privacy of your meditation room, place your arms down at your side. Then, mentally chanting *AUM*, bring them upward, straight out to the side, with your palms up, until you join the palms high above the head. Mentally create an aura of upward-moving light around your body.

6) Extend your arms before you, your palms touching. Then move them out and around your body in a broad circle until the palms or fingers touch once again behind your back. Mentally, while repeating this process, chant, "AUM-TAT-SAT." (The *a*'s in TAT-SAT are pronounced short, with an "uh" sound: "TUT-SUT.") Repeat this process at least three times. After you've finished it, feel yourself surrounded by that protective vibration.

7) Try not to look into the eyes of, or shake hands with, people whose vibrations are negative. This avoidance may prove a little socially awkward at times so I don't insist on it, but I should state that these are two of the strongest ways by which magnetism is exchanged between people. (This is one little-known reason for the palms-folded greeting, the *namaskar*, which Indians customarily use in place of the handshake.)

8) When you find that you must enter a disharmonious environment, keep a spiritual "bodyguard" with you: someone who is on the same spiritual wavelength as you, to help keep your magnetism strong.

9) If you feel yourself under psychic attack from anyone, use your thumb to place a cross of blue light mentally on the attacker. Do it with sufficient will power, and harmful energy will be unable to reach you, but will return to its sender. Direct good energy along with the blocking energy, that your attacker be cured of his anger. A *mantra* to repeat in such circumstances is *"AUM hreeng kleeng Krishnaya namaha."* (The first *a* in Krishnaya is pronounced as in our "ah." The other *a*'s are pronounced as in "uh.")

Good company, as I said, is extremely important on the spiritual path. Seek out the company of others of like mind. Mix with them lovingly. If you know someone whose spiritual magnetism is particularly strong, spend time with that person. If outward good company is not available, keep good company mentally.

One of the best ways of surrounding yourself with good vibrations is to listen to uplifting music.

Most important of all, try to keep the company of saints. They will help you, even from a distance, by their subtle magnetic influence. If you know no such people, read their lives; visit places where they have lived; mix with those who knew them. If possible, listen to recordings of their voices.

Be conscious, above all, of your own developing magnetism. Feel it surrounding you as you walk, flowing through you as you converse with others. Expand it to the people in your vicinity; include them in your aura.

The more you act as a channel of blessing to others, the more you yourself will be blessed. Your magnetism will be enhanced, and your efforts to reach God greatly accelerated.

****

MEDITATION EXERCISE

Set the photograph of some great saint or master before you. Not a painting, merely: a photograph. Gaze intently into his or her eyes. Attune yourself to the magnetism you feel there.

After some time, close your eyes in meditation and try to feel a response in your heart. Feel yourself bathed and uplifted by that person's superconsciousness.

Then pray deeply: "Draw me closer to God."

Chapter Thirteen

CHANTING
AND AFFIRMATIONS

"Chanting is half the battle," said Paramhansa Yogananda.

Words are thoughts crystallized. Melodies are the resonance of the heart's aspirations. Harmonies deepen the emotional power of those aspirations. And rhythms ground those aspirations in the present. Combining thought, melody, and rhythm in a spiritual discipline can provide a powerful force for awakening. This force must be used rightly, for just as it can be used to uplift, so can it also harm or debase.

During the time of Nazi Germany, highly effective, although negative, use was made of slogans, melodies, rhythms, and harmonies that entered the subconscious, influencing normally pleasant but suggestible people and sweeping them along on a tidal wave of mass hysteria and hate.

Chants can be powerful in a number of ways. Sri Ramakrishna, the great master, met a man who had a reputation for being a fierce disputant. In debate, the man was unbeatable. Ramakrishna was shown in meditation that this man's success was due to a certain *mantra* (a powerful word-formula) that he repeated before every verbal encounter. Upon meeting him, and before the man could utter his *mantra,* Sri Ramakrishna repeated it loudly. The man was thereby stripped of his power, and lost his aggressiveness and conceit.

Another example of the power of *mantra* comes from the life of Paramhansa Yogananda, when he stilled a violent wind. The wind was a manifestation, he declared later, of the karma of World War II: in other words, of the energy that had been stirred up by the violence of that war. He recalled a *mantra* he'd learned as a child in India, and asked a disciple to repeat it while striking three times with her shoe on the porch where they were standing. Instantly, the wind subsided. An article appeared the next day in the *Los Angeles Times* commenting on the strong wind that had begun blowing the day before, and then, suddenly, subsided.

In a Yucatan jungle in Mexico, over forty years ago, I asked my guide if he had ever witnessed a rain dance.

"It is interesting you should ask that," he replied. "As it happens, I was in this area once, years ago, when the land was experiencing a severe drought. I came upon a village where, in the *zocalo* (town square), I saw a rain dance being performed. I stood for a time, watching the dancers. All of a sudden, out of a clear blue sky, dark clouds gathered. Moments later we were drenched in a great downpour."

I knew of a man in India who had a *mantra* to cure cobra bites. He worked in a telegraph office. Telegrams arrived there frequently from remote parts of the country, requesting cures. The effectiveness of his cure was legendary.

The power of *mantra*s and chanting doesn't come automatically. Will power and concentration are needed, and inner attunement with the words.

The spiritual purpose of chanting is not to develop powers, but to give one control over the mind, that he may direct it one-pointedly toward God. If chants and *mantra*s can bestow power over objective nature, how much greater their effectiveness when their aim is to benefit the chanter himself. The highest purpose of chanting is to help awaken us to our own spiritual potential: to bring us closer to Self-realization.

Spiritual chanting is heartfelt prayer, deepened by the dimension of music and by the building power of repetition. Repetition is not for the purpose of getting the Lord's attention: It is to deepen the intensity of one's own prayer. To repeat a chant mechanically, in a singsong manner, has virtually no spiritual value.

Spiritual chanting is different from singing songs or hymns. I've written well over a hundred songs myself—for instruction, inspiration, and reflection. Such music serves a different purpose, however. Though it may inspire, it doesn't lift the mind into a meditative state.

HOW TO CHANT

The art of chanting correctly is, first, to practice it with full awareness of its *inner* purpose. That purpose is not to awaken sentiments or to stir up the emotions. It is to focus the heart's feelings and raise them toward superconsciousness.

The Maharani of Cooch Behar told me she'd once asked her family priest why he intoned his chants so loudly. "Well, you see, your Highness," he explained, "God is far away. If I don't shout, how will He hear me?" God isn't far away, of course. It is we who distance our-selves from Him by the "noise" in our own minds, a noise people often carry with them into their prayers and meditations.

Loud chanting does have its place. It is good at the start of meditation—not for the reason that priest gave, but to command attention from our own minds. For loud chanting creates a magnetic flow. Like a mighty river, it can dissolve the eddies of thought and feeling that meander idly along the banks of the mind. Like a magnetic military leader, it commands attention from your thought-soldiers and fires them with zeal.

Once you've got their attention, chant more softly, more inwardly. Direct your energy upward, now, from the heart to the Spiritual Eye.

Once your conscious mind is wholly engaged in chanting, bring it down into the subconscious by whis-pering. While chanting in the subconscious, offer the chant there, too, up to superconsciousness at the point between the eyebrows, until you feel your entire being vibrating with the words, the melody, and the rhythm.

At last, chant only mentally, at the point between the eyebrows. Let your absorption lift you into supercon-sciousness. Once it does so, and once you receive a divine response, you will have spiritualized the chant.

From then on, any time you sing the chant it will quickly carry you again to superconsciousness as if on a magic carpet.

To spiritualize a chant, keep it rotating in the mind— for days at a time, if necessary: not only in meditation, but as you go about your daily activities. This practice is also called *japa*. Christian mystics, too, speak of the continuous "prayer of the heart," and of "practicing the presence of God." All this is *japa*.

The higher aspect of chanting involves listening to the mighty sound of *AUM,* and becoming absorbed in it. You'll hear this sound first in the right ear. Gradually let it permeate the brain and the entire body, until every cell vibrates with that sound. After that, try to hear *AUM* in everything you do, in everything you perceive. This is true *japa,* when the mind no longer repeats words, merely, but is intoxicated with the bliss of the "music of the spheres."

The Cosmic Sound is described variously in the world's scriptures. The Jews and Christians call it the *Amen.* Muslims call it the *Amin.* To the Zoroastrians it is *Ahunavar.* To Hindus and Buddhists it is *AUM.* In the first chapter of the Gospel of St. John, the Cosmic Vibration is called the Word: "In the beginning was the Word, and the Word was with God, and the Word *was* God."

The word *AUM* is an attempt to capture in human speech the sound of the Cosmic Vibration. By attuning one's consciousness to that sound (by Christians called also the Holy Ghost and the Comforter), one enters the stream of vibration that proceeded out of the Spirit, and that merges back into the Spirit at creation's end and at

181

the end of the individual soul's cycle of outward wandering. By merging in *AUM,* liberation is attained.

Once the mind is focused by chanting, and the inner energy is awakened, take your chanting inward. Don't only "make a glad noise unto the Lord," as the Bible puts it: *Listen* for His answer. Meditation *is* listening, as I've said. Feel yourself chanting in attunement, above all, with the Cosmic Sound. Harmonize yourself inwardly with that sound.

Harmony is an aspect of music not usually included in traditional chanting. In the West, where harmony is so intrinsic to musical expression, one may wonder if the lack of harmony in Eastern music is not due simply to a lack of musical sophistication. I recall the first time I heard spiritual chanting. I'd been raised on Bach, Mozart, Beethoven, and other classical Western composers. I'd also studied singing in the Western classical tradition. Compared to that music, the stark simplicity of chanting seemed to me almost naive.

It was only when I got deeply into it that I understood its spiritual power. And it is only since composing music myself, complete with harmonies, that I appreciate more fully the fact that, although harmony lends richness and emotional depth to music, its very complexity prevents it from bringing melody into deeper harmony with *AUM.*

Even though I try, in my own music, to write chords that will help the mind to flow in an upward direction, I am well aware that the true "music of the spheres" lies far beyond outer harmonies. It creates another kind of harmony in the soul.

What Words to Use?

There is not a strong tradition of chanting in the West. Most of the chanting I've heard has been Gregorian chant, which is little heard outside of monasteries, or chants transported from India. Buddhist chanting, like Gregorian chant, is a recitation of scripture and is not, therefore, an appeal of the heart to God. The Indian form of chanting usually involves repeating various names of God. Since these names are foreign to most Westerners, and don't possess the deep emotional associations they have for most Indians, they are less deeply meaningful, in themselves, than they are for people who grew up in India, or else are not always meaningful in the same way.

I suspect that for most Westerners the words have more a *mantric* influence than a sentimental appeal. The sounds uplift, but the words are less easily associated in the Western mind than in the Indian with mental images of Rama with his bow, Sita in her selfless service to Rama, Krishna with his flute, Ganesha with his elephant's head, and so on. The extreme antiquity of Hindu culture has guaranteed an abundance of symbols, most of which have lost their inner meanings even for Hindus. The lack of such visual associations with the names may, in one way, be an advantage for Westerners, since it forces them to focus more on the sounds of the names, as they allow those vibrations, which are powerful, to uplift them.

Other aspects of the Indian chants—the melodies and the rhythms—are often soul-stirring, and need no further explanation. India has developed a tradition of chanting as an expression of deep, intimate love for God. There is power in such chanting, even if you don't really relate to the words you're singing.

Paramhansa Yogananda, as a great yogi whose mission was to disseminate the yoga teachings in the West, introduced a new kind of chanting here. It is based on the repetition of meaningful phrases, rather than of the divine names. Some of the chants he wrote he translated from Bengali or Hindi songs. Others, he wrote himself. This kind of chanting is more like a repetitive prayer set to music, and is better suited for meditators, who understand the importance of combining the soul's appeal for divine grace with self-effort. For by singing God's names only, what remains in the mind is the thought "God will do it all for me." What Yogananda's method of chanting accomplishes is to awaken in the mind the thought "In these ways I will cooperate with His grace."

One of his chants goes:

> I am the bubble, make me the sea.
> So do Thou, my Lord! Thou and I, never apart,
> Wave of the sea dissolve in the sea,
> I am the bubble, make me the sea.

Very simple, you see? And very easily memorized. When such a chant is sung repeatedly, the mind is easily lifted up into meditation.

Some of Paramhansa Yogananda's chants go further in the direction of personal affirmation, and are less similar to the traditional concept of prayer. An example of such a chant begins with these words:

Why, O mind, wanderest thou?
Go in thine inner home!

These chants, too, are powerful, spiritualized as they were by a great master. They are in many ways better suited for people who follow the path of meditation. I myself have sung them for as long as I've been meditating—nearly fifty years. The inspiration I derive from them is precious to me beyond words.

AFFIRMATIONS

Yogananda's chants lead naturally to another aspect of this subject that relates deeply also to meditation as a means for self-improvement. He explained that there is a connection between two traditionally opposite teachings. Much religious teaching avers that one can do nothing to uplift oneself: One can only wait for God's grace to descend. Other teachings, notably in Buddhism, aver exactly the opposite—that man must do the whole work of upliftment himself, without the benefit of grace.

Yogananda brought these two teachings together into a harmonious whole. He explained that we should use "our own, but God-given power." God, in other words, doesn't do all the work for us, but neither can we do it all alone.

Earlier, I used the illustration of a sounding board, which enables a violin sound to fill a concert hall. For people of less devotional nature, who are more attracted by the thought of self-effort, this image of the sounding board is important. For nobody exists in psychic isolation.

The thought, which some people propound, that everything we see is a projection of our own consciousness, is easily contradicted by one simple example: Our consciousness could never have manifested the hundreds of languages spoken in the world! A person is considered a linguist if he speaks only three or four. The universe, in other words, is indeed a projection of consciousness, but of Pure Consciousness, not of our little human brains. The Greater Mind of which we are but a small part—and by no means an executive part at that, except where our own lives are concerned—projected everything into existence.

Where we ourselves are concerned, our role in transforming our consciousness is significant. Affirmation is one way to involve ourselves in this process. Without personal involvement, divine grace won't keep us from drifting downstream helplessly like a scattering of fallen petals.

Affirmations should be positive, rhythmic, and forceful. Never, for instance, make negative affirmations such as "I'm not ill." The operative declaration to your subconscious must not be that word "ill." Affirm then, instead, "I am well!"

Melodies aren't generally used when making affirmations, though they may be, and can also prove helpful. Normally, however, affirmations are spoken, not sung. Thus, for affirmation, we have words and rhythm. Rhythm in affirmations is especially important, as it must compensate for the omission of melody.

Select word formulae, or create them, to uplift the mind on wing-beats of a suitable rhythm. Here, for instance, is an affirmation that I used when my heart was giving me trouble:

> Thy light pervades my body cells:
> Thy light pervades my heart.
> Thy light perfects my body cells:
> Thy light perfects my heart.

Affirmations, like chanting, should be uttered out loud, then more softly, then in a whisper, then silently, then ever more superconsciously at the point between the eyebrows, until they imbue your entire being with their force and meaning.

The best times to repeat affirmations are when the subconscious is naturally open: the moment of awaking in the morning, and just before falling asleep at night.

Paramhansa Yogananda's little book *Scientific Healing Affirmations** is a classic in this genre. Read it for helpful affirmations. I also wrote a book several years ago, *Affirmations for Self-Healing*. Here is an affirmation from that book on the subject of God-remembrance: "I will live in the remembrance of what I am in truth: bliss infinite! eternal love!"

The important thing to bear in mind is that, because the mind has a tendency to use words while thinking, it is helpful to use them in such a way as to uplift the mind in cooperation with divine inspiration.

Again, consciously or subliminally people tend to recognize in melodic structure the essence of heart feeling. Guide your feelings, then, in a positive direction by singing uplifting melodies.

---

*Los Angeles: Self-Realization Fellowship, 1981.

We tend also to ground our consciousness by rhythm. Support your chanting and affirmations, therefore, with rhythms that help to awaken and strengthen your determination to go deeper in meditation. Most of the rhythms one hears in music nowadays are degrading— literally so, for they magnetize the lower *chakras* in such a way as to draw the energy downward. Grounding rhythms should uplift, not grind one into the ground!

A final but very important point: After chanting, especially, but also after making affirmations, sit silently as long as you can do so with joy. Meditate. Chanting is, indeed, only a preparation for meditation. Not to use it as a send-off into silence is to leave the airplane after taxiing it onto the runway.

****

MEDITATION EXERCISE

Imagine a choir composed of every atom in the universe, each one an individual, but all of them singing together in blissful harmony.

In your own mind, join that mighty choir, composed of all life. Determine from today on to sing in harmony with the universe. Don't impose on the great anthem of life your little wishes for how you want the music to sound. Unite your notes to that Infinite Sound.

The more you do so, the more deeply you will know yourself to be an expression of the soaring anthem of Infinity.

Chapter Fourteen

GOD — PERSONAL OR IMPERSONAL?

It is difficult to imagine Pure Consciousness—undifferentiated, absolute. It is harder still to address prayers to that unimaginable state of being. And if you meditate on it, on what do you focus your mind? On nothingness?

Not only is it virtually impossible to meditate on nothingness: There are inherent dangers in even attempting to do so. For although, to go deep in meditation, you must empty the mind of thoughts, you must at the same time be deeply aware, inwardly—of the inner peace, for example. To make the mind blank is to open oneself passively to every vibratory influence in one's environment. Mental blankness doesn't even help one to receive whatever good influences there are: It opens one only to the negative ones. The way to make yourself receptive to higher vibrations is to raise your consciousness to their vibratory level.

Rather than meditating on nothingness, if that impersonal direction suits you, meditate on the thought of freedom from "anythingness." Soul-freedom is a positive concept. Stillness is a positive concept. Perfect peace and calmness are positive concepts. Blankness is not. Always keep your consciousness moving in the direction of *more,* not less, awareness.

If, after meditation, you find yourself wondering vaguely, "Where was I?" the chances are you were slipping into subconsciousness, not rising toward superconsciousness. There comes a point in meditation where peace steals over the mind, but then, because of our long association of restfulness with sleep, the mind tends to drift off into a quasi-dream state. At that time, make an extra effort of will to rise toward superconsciousness. Concentrate with extra intensity at the point between the eyebrows, the seat of will power and of superconscious ecstasy.

There is, as I've said earlier, a fine line between the conscious state and the subconscious. Superconsciousness exists in another dimension altogether; it is not, like the other two states, a part of human consciousness. That line represents the reduction of our three-dimensional universe to one dimension. If you can penetrate that fine line mentally, you will find yourself able to slip easily into superconsciousness. Because the line *is* a fine one, however, it is easy to miss it when the mind arrives at its first glimpse of inner peace. At that point, take care lest you slip down into a vague in-between state—a sort of conscious subconsciousness.

In this state it is possible to see hallucinations, which rise from the subconscious. Don't mistake those images for true visions. Hallucinations are an obstacle on the spiritual path. Don't fall into the trap of thinking that they represent guidance from above.

SUPERCONSCIOUSNESS, OR SUBCONSCIOUSNESS?

How to distinguish between the two? The first and most important way is to see the effect of your inner experience on your everyday life. Has there been a definite change for the better? Superconscious experience, which includes true visions, will do that for you; hallucinations will not. Be honest with yourself: Don't look only at the short-range effects: Look at the long range. People naturally want to believe that their visions were true; they may affirm changes in themselves that seem real to them, temporarily. Time, then, will tell whether the change has proved lasting and real.

Another way is to observe your *underlying* consciousness during the experience. Is it intensely peaceful? Is it in fact superconscious? Or is it more or less commonplace? Is the light brilliant within which the vision appears, or is it clouded and dull? If a person in your vision speaks to you, do the words inspire you with a more expanded consciousness, or do they draw your mind downward to your ego?

A vitally important test also is this: Is the teaching you've received in harmony with the highest spiritual traditions of the ages? Or does it challenge them? Does it support and respect those teachings, or does it, if referring to them, speak with condescension or familiarity?

For, beyond hallucinations, there are also delusive (because false) manifestations of lower astral entities that can masquerade as angels or great masters, but that have no other aim than to trick you into taking a downward path. Such entities may look beautiful, and may inspire you because of your very desire for a true vision. They will tend, however, to flatter you and make you feel that you are on equal standing with the greatest souls, even if, in your outer life, you are still prone to such human emotions as selfishness, anger, and desire.

Don't be discouraged by such manifestations. Their very coming signifies a certain degree of spiritual progress on your part—even as, if a con man shows interest in you, it probably means you've enough wealth to attract his interest. Confidence tricks, however, work only on people who have the failing of avarice to be worked on. A person who is not interested in quick money-making schemes can't be conned. And a meditator who has no interest in having his ego flattered cannot be fooled by lower astral entities, whose only interest is in drawing people back to ego-consciousness. Such souls, locked in their own misery, hate to see someone spurning the falsehood to which they themselves cling as their abiding reality—ego, the root cause of their misery.

Above all, don't be attached to the idea of having visions. Don't seek them. If they come to you, and if you believe them to be true, be divinely grateful for them, but remember that they, as well as any other experience you receive, belong to God; they are not your possessions. Behold in any vision, then, the consciousness of

192

infinity. If you see a human form, behold the infinite consciousness lambent in its eyes.

For Pure Consciousness, which is God, will be subtly present behind any true vision that you see. You may have a vision of Jesus, for example, or of the Madonna; or you may see Krishna, or the Buddha: Remember, souls that are in God have no ego to separate them from infinite consciousness. If Jesus comes to you, it is not Jesus the man you will see, but Pure Consciousness in the form of Jesus. I don't at all mean that Pure Consciousness will be tricking you into believing you are seeing something that isn't really there. I mean that that is what Jesus was even while he lived on earth. Like all great masters, he had transcended his ego and realized himself as Infinite Consciousness. As Paramhansa Yogananda put it, "I killed Yogananda long ago. No one dwells in this temple now but God." And so it seemed to me, whenever I looked into his eyes. There was no human personality there with likes and dislikes and other normal egoic reactions.

What you see in vision, then, will be Jesus (or the Madonna, or Buddha, or Krishna, or Yogananda) as he was on earth, with all the memory of that incarnation; but you will behold him self-transcended, calling you from infinity to embrace him in infinity.

A Personal God

God, you see, is personal in His relationship with you because *you* are personal. He descends to your level in order to draw you up to His. What He calls you to is, ultimately, the impersonality of Pure Consciousness.

At the same time, He is conscious of you, individually. Where your own consciousness is concerned, He *is* you. If the divine center were missing in any atom of creation, it could not exist anywhere. The divine consciousness is "center everywhere, circumference nowhere." It is as conscious of you, individually, as it is of the very galaxy through which our little planet whirls.

This is not merely a matter of philosophical speculation. It is what the soul discovers in meditation. It is the testimony of great masters who have found God.

When you pray to God, whatever your religion, pray deeply, and you will receive an answer. Because Christians may have visions of Jesus, and Hindus, visions of Krishna, they may claim respectively that God Himself endorses Jesus over Krishna, or Krishna over Jesus. God, meanwhile, smiles at humanity through all forms, even through the rocks. In Self-realized masters He appears openly, but all outer forms are but filters for Pure Consciousness.

Is God really conscious of us, personally? Is He conscious of our thoughts, our feelings, our human needs? Of course He is! He knows every flicker of your thoughts. He *is* you!

And He can appear to you in any form that you hold dear. Years ago, someone tried to convert me to his own concept of God. I tried to open his mind to other concepts, but he would have none of it.

Finally I said to him, "Let's face it, no matter what you and I think about these matters, we are both wrong! Our little human experience can't possibly prepare us for infinite understanding."

Anandamoyee Ma would sometimes put it this way (to clarify matters!): "It is and it isn't, and neither is it nor is it not."

Friend,—

> Do you seek to escape Him in activity?
> You cannot, for He is there.
> Do you seek refuge from Him in sensuality?
> You cannot, for He is also there.
> Do you seek to avoid Him in mental restlessness?
> You cannot, for He is your very restlessness.
> Though you try to forget Him,
> Never will He forget you.
> For you are not even you: *He* is you!

God will come to you, when the magnetism of your devotion grows strong enough to attract Him through the filter of your expectations and desires. It is not important how you define Him: Any definition you give will be for *your* satisfaction; it will never limit Him. All that matters is that you love Him.

Him—Her—It. What does it matter? He is all that. He is also nothing—that is to say, no thing. Find that form which satisfies not so much your philosophical mind as your heart's longing.

Personally, I prefer to think of God as my Divine Mother. So also did Yogananda. "The Mother," he would say, "is closer than the Father. If you err, the Mother won't spank you. She will forgive you always, and will always try to help you."

A man, hauled before the court, was once asked, "How do you plead?"—in other words, guilty or not guilty.

"Your honor," the man cried, "Ah pleads for mercy!"

Think of God in that aspect which makes you feel loved, not judged—which makes you relaxed, not fearful. For only in relaxation is there peace. And only in inner peace is spiritual progress assured.

There is a sweetness in an "I-and-Thou" relationship with God that is lost when one tries too hard to be philosophically correct. The highest reality is, in fact, *advaitic,* or non-dualistic. Duality comes into manifestation with cosmic creation. In duality, there is a natural polar opposite to everything. But there isn't the sweetness, as human beings understand it, in a love that has nothing outside itself to love—in a love that is, itself, the very thing it loves.

Even masters, Paramhansa Yogananda used to say, enjoy descending the ladder of consciousness from time to time, to enjoy once again the relationship of "I" and "Thou."

****

MEDITATION EXERCISE

Visualize a great ocean of light—nothing but brilliant, pure, golden light everywhere.

Feel that the little ripples on the ocean are ripples of peace, drawing your restless mind into new, delightful rhythms filled with happiness and understanding.

Now visualize, slowly rising out of the ocean depths, that particular form of God which you yourself hold most dear. As it rises, see that it, too, is composed of light. It rises from the ocean, and belongs to the ocean. Claim it, if you will, as your own, but know that it belongs to that ocean of light. It is yours to the extent that you recognize that light also as your own.

Visualize that divinely beautiful form calling you— not to itself, but to that radiant, golden light, which it would share with you.

To be embraced by that form is to be embraced by that light.

Open your heart, and, with deep love, surrender everything you have, everything you are, to that infinity of peace and light.

Chapter Fifteen

INTERIORIZING THE MIND

My guru said to me, "Always remain in the Self. Come down a little every now and then to eat or talk, as necessary. Then withdraw into the Self again."

Nothing meaningful is accomplished by accident. There must be awareness in the act; the greater the awareness, the more meaningful the act itself. Poets and other artists may persuade themselves that they inject meaning into works by making them "significantly" vague. Their public, too, may profess to find meaning in such works. If, however, you ask them, "What meaning?" they, too, become "significantly" vague. One can project meaning onto a rock if one is so inclined, but for any such projection the rock itself deserves no credit.

Many meditators hope to progress spiritually by going through the prescribed motions, even if their minds are engaged elsewhere. Form, unfortunately for dilettantes, is no substitute for content. There are no magic formulae to do the work of meditation for you. You must do it yourself. God Himself won't draw you to Him unless you participate actively in the process.

The purpose of meditation is to help you to enter the inner "kingdom of God." Meditation practices can do much for you, but only if your mind longs to go within. No technique will take you to God automatically.

Interiorization of the mind is essential. This fifth stage on the path of meditation (*pratyahara* in Sanskrit) can be perfected only after *pranayama,* the fourth stage, which brings the energy-flow in the body under control. As is true at every stage of the spiritual path, however, there is a homogeneity in the various stages that requires us to see the whole of it in every part—as much so at the beginning as at the end.

The time to begin interiorizing your mind, then, is as soon as you set foot on the path in earnest. Without interiorization, you'll never be able to practice any of its stages successfully. And your meditations will never achieve fruition.

There must come a time on the path when former attractions no longer seem attractive; when life's excitements, its gains and its losses, simply don't matter any more; when people's opinions, including your own, become quite irrelevant to you; and when the only thing that matters is to remain in the peace and joy of your own being. Even if this attitude seems foreign to you at present, it will flower someday of its own accord in your mind, if you work now at interiorizing your mind. For you will realize that you are complete in yourself; that within you lies everything you once sought so ardently outside yourself.

To work at achieving wisdom, don't wait for it to come to you—as a kind of prize for having meditated. Interiorization is not only a state one achieves: It is an attitude that must be cultivated conscientiously throughout the journey.

Try to relate everything you see and do to the inner Self. When you behold a beautiful flower, try to sense the essence of its beauty in the Self. When hearing beautiful music, try to hear its source in the music of the soul; listen with the inner ear—inside the right ear, especially. When eating good food, try to taste it at the point between the eyebrows.

Draw every sense enjoyment inward, that you enjoy it at your own highest center. This attitude is, in its own way, as important for the meditator as meditation itself.

Non-Involvement

To prepare the mind for deep interiorization, which is true *pratyahara,* practice what is known in Sanskrit as *titiksha.* The best, though not an ideal, translation of this word into English is "endurance." To complete the meaning, add to it two more concepts: evenmindedness, and inward non-involvement. The underlying attitude of the meditator should be, "I am evenminded and cheerful under all circumstances." Let nothing draw you too much out of yourself. *Titiksha* should become for you a basic life-attitude.

If the weather is cold, mentally resist that sensation. Be sensible, of course: Put on something warm, unless your mind is strong enough to resist the cold. But don't cry out even mentally, "Brrrrr, how cold it is!"

If the weather is warm, remove your jacket, if you like, but don't allow the thought "I can't stand this heat!" to agitate your mind.

If you experience physical pain, do what you wish to relieve the discomfort, but at the same time resist it mentally. Tell yourself, smiling, "A little pain never hurt anyone!" And affirm, "I am Spirit! I am not this body."

The same holds true for the experience of emotional pain. Accept it calmly. Don't allow it to enslave you to outwardness by reacting to it on its own emotional level. Tell yourself firmly, "In my Self I remain eternally untouched."

You will find it easier to remain unaffected by pain of any kind if you can remain calm also during the experience of pleasure. In little ways and in great, remind yourself constantly, "No outer circumstance affects who I am, inside."

I have made it a point in my own life to practice *titiksha* even in ordinary circumstances: while eating a good meal, or while seated in a dentist's chair (where, using *titiksha* as a substitute for novocain, I've affirmed inner freedom). By so doing I don't diminish the pleasure of a delicious meal: I simply transfer the focus of that enjoyment to the inner Self. And I don't dull my senses by not giving in to pain: I simply relax from the pain, or else expand my consciousness to include that sensation in a broader, more commanding awareness.

One gratifying result of meditation is that it increases one's capacity also for sensory enjoyment. Sounds become more entrancing; beautiful sights, more thrillingly beautiful; pleasant tastes, more utterly delicious. It is hedonists, not yogis, whose senses become jaded.

On the other hand, pleasures have less power to enslave the mind with the practice of *titiksha*. You can switch off the sensations, mentally, whenever you like, so that even if you place a delicacy on your tongue, you won't taste it.

Practice mental freedom under all circumstances and you'll find yourself gaining the ability to rise not only above pleasure, but above pain also.

The practice of *titiksha* teaches many useful lessons. For example, you'll learn that pleasure and pain exist only in the mind. If you accept them impartially, without defining them as something that ought, or ought not, to be, you'll attain that state of inner equanimity from which you'll derive unceasing happiness.

A Lesson in Acceptance

I had an interesting lesson in acceptance years ago. I was scheduled to give a series of lectures in Kuranda, near the city of Cairns, in Australia, and was returning to the mainland from the Great Barrier Reef. The night before this program was to begin, I stayed on Green Island, sixteen miles off the coast. The weather had been ideal. For my return, however, the weather turned wretched. Were two hundred people, I wondered, going to be silent witnesses to my struggle against the lingering effects of seasickness?

I'd never been a good sailor. As a child I'd crossed the Atlantic several times with my parents, and though I loved the sea (discounting the first day or two), bad weather had always been, for me, a martyrdom. Every time the ship's prow rose above the horizon, I'd strain mentally to pull it down again. Every time it sank below the horizon, I'd struggle mentally to pull it back up. As I left Green Island, I resolved to approach this lifelong problem in a new way.

The sea seemed to be shouting gleefully, "You ain't seen nothin' yet!" But every time the ship lurched, heaved, and staggered with corkscrew motions through towering waves, I exclaimed determinedly, "Wonderful! This is just how it *should* be!" My arrival at Cairns left me a bit drained of will power, but otherwise in great shape.

EVENMINDEDNESS

Life provides us with countless opportunities to practice evenmindedness. We should be grateful for them. We should be grateful even for mental or emotional setbacks, or for circumstances that conspire to make us look ridiculous. As for the latter, laugh them off! Nothing is, after all, permanently bad.

There is a technique for interiorizing the mind that I've used in the dentist's chair, and on many other occasions when my body was experiencing pain. It is actually an important technique for deepening one's meditations, but it illustrates also how these meditation practices can be applied to outer situations as well. By so applying them, we develop attitudes that further assist our meditative efforts also.

This technique involves the repetition of a *mantra*. (I discussed this word two chapters ago.) The *mantra* has a vibratory connection with the breath, through its resonance in the medulla oblongata, which controls the breath (as well as the pulse rate and the blood pressure). The medulla oblongata, as I said earlier, is the seat of ego-consciousness. And the spiritual path may be defined as a process of transcending ego-consciousness in the realization of our true Self: the soul.

The *mantra,* in Sanskrit, means "I am He"—that is to say, "I am Spirit." To give it special power, however, it is pronounced somewhat differently from the normal Sanskrit to enhance its vibratory efficacy.

The Sanskrit words are "*Aham* (I) *Saha* (He)."* As a *mantra,* however, the words are pronounced "*Hong Sau*" (*Sau* to be pronounced like the English word, "saw"). "*Hong,*" like the tolling of a bell, rings outward as though dissolving the sound into the surrounding atmosphere. This reverberation merges into Spirit with the next sound, "*Sau.*" The sound "*Sau*" emphasizes the consciousness of peace. "*Hong*" vibrates with the incoming breath; "*Sau,*" with the outgoing. The two sounds together bring our breathing gradually into a state of peace and equilibrium.

There is a subtle connection between the physical breath and the movement of energy in the astral body. For along the spine, on either side of it, run the two ganglionated cords of the sympathetic nervous system. These cords have their counterpart in the astral body, where they are known in the yoga teachings as *iḍa* (on the left side of the spine) and *pingala* (on the right side).

*I've added an *a* at the end of *saha,* as is often done, to make it clear that it is pronounced with the *h* aspirated, and not like an Englishman's version of "sir."

When we inhale, there is a corresponding upward movement of energy in the *iḍa* nerve channel. When we exhale, there is a downward movement in the *pingala.*

There is a correspondence also between this energy-flow and our emotional reactions. When we react happily to anything, the energy flows upward through *ida,* and at the same time we inhale. When we react unhappily, the energy flows downward through *pingala,* and we exhale.

You can easily test the relationship between your emotional reactions and the breath. For isn't your first reaction to good news likely to be a deep inhalation? And isn't your first reaction to bad news likely to be a sigh? The matter is more complex than that, of course. For example, bad news may cause an inhalation, not an exhalation, if our reaction to it is to rise determinedly to combat the bad news. Good news, on the contrary, may cause us to exhale if we greet it with a feeling of relief—with the thought, for example, "Well, thank God that's over!"

With rising energy on inhalation, in other words, there is also an affirmation of outward involvement. With descending energy on exhalation, there is also a withdrawal from outward involvement, not necessarily accompanied by feelings of sadness or depression.

Iḍa and *pingala* are the channels of reactive energy. That energy is superficial. *Within* the spine is what is known as the *sushumna,* where an upward flow of energy leads to spiritual awakening.

By centering our consciousness in the superficial spine (the *iḍa* and *pingala*), we concentrate our likes and dislikes there where our thoughts and emotions manifest their reactions to outer circumstances. These reactions carry the mind outward by focusing its attention on the circumstances instead of inwardly, on the reactions themselves.

As we retrace pleasure and pain back from outer effect to inner cause—to the reactive process itself in its place of origin in the spine—we learn to control our involvement in the ups and downs of life. We develop equanimity thereby, instead of projecting likes and dislikes onto a world we can do little to improve anyway. Instead of thinking, for instance, "Oh, how wonderful that we're going on an outing!" or "How I hate having to go to work today!" we calm the reactive process in ourselves and thus remain always peaceful and happy, regardless of outer circumstances.

For to react positively is still to react, and by so doing to identify ourselves with outwardness. Because the universe, moreover, is founded on duality, every positive reaction must perforce be succeeded by a negative one; every ascent in the superficial spine through *ida* must be succeeded by a downward movement through *pingala*—even as a ball, thrown into the air, must come down again. The yogi learns, instead, to be inwardly always "evenminded and cheerful."

Interestingly, by the very act of calming our emotional reactions to circumstances, we find ourselves able to influence outer circumstances far more than people do who dance unceasingly in reaction to them.

Thus, *titiksha* doesn't make one apathetic or dull. It isn't that you don't allow yourself to enjoy anything. Rather, you live at the source of enjoyment in yourself.

Once the reactive process has been stilled, you find joy welling up constantly in the deep spine. It is a joy that, because it exists in the Self and not outwardly in duality, has no neutralizing opposite.

An attitude of *titiksha* is the first step to interiorizing the mind, and to bringing its reactions under control. To practice *titiksha,* concentrate on your reactions to things rather than on the things you think cause the reactions. Don't "run riot" with your feelings. Tell yourself, when fortune smiles, that no good thing lasts forever; and again, when misfortune frowns, that misfortune is never unalloyed or permanent.

An important way of practicing *titiksha* is to watch the breath. By retracing this reactive process from the periphery of awareness ever more deeply to our center in the spine, we develop that mind-set which ultimately brings us to *pratyahara:* interiorization of the mind.

THE FIFTH STAGE: *PRATYAHARA*

The process of *pratyahara* begins with observation of the breath. Awareness of the breath is traced back to the corresponding movements of energy in the spine. Gradually, the breath becomes calm, and the reactive energies are brought under control. As the meditator ceases mentally to dance the jig of life's ups and downs, he develops centeredness in the inner Self. It is after this point is reached that meditation, properly so called, can begin.

In *The Rubaiyat of Omar Khayyam Explained,** Paramhansa Yogananda makes an extraordinary statement

***Op. cit.,* Stanza Thirty-One.

regarding the inner world of the soul. After describing the interrelationship of the mind and body through the nerves, he writes:

"As the life-force moves down the spine and out to the body and its senses, the mind is drawn outward also. Sense-stimulation from within impels one to seek fulfillment in sense-pleasures.

"The same nervous system, however, constitutes *the one and only path* to spiritual enlightenment, regardless of formal religious affiliation. When the energy can be coaxed to reverse its flow from the senses to the brain, it reveals to our consciousness another world."

I began this discussion by mentioning how the *mantra "Hong-Sau,"* can be used to dissolve the consciousness of pain. All pain originates in the thought of ego ("Why is this happening to *me?*"). By mentally chanting *"Hong-Sau"* at the seat of that pain, one dissolves the ego's connection to the pain, and thereby lessens, or even dissolves, the pain itself.

Try doing this while you sit in the dentist's chair (I mention the dentist's chair because it was my first example), or at any other time that you experience pain, whether physically, mentally, or emotionally. Don't limit your practice to those times when you want desperately to rise above pain. Do it in response to any sensation, whether light or intense, pleasant or unpleasant, simply as an exercise in interiorization of the mind.

Concentrate at the center of the sensation. Then *watch* the breath at that center. Don't control the breath. Simply watch it. As it comes in of its own accord, follow it mentally with the chant *Hong.* Feel as you do so that the word itself is relaxing and dissolving your ego-identification with that sensation.

Then, as the breath flows out, follow it mentally with the chant *Sau*. Feel, with the utterance of this word, that you are coming ever more deeply to rest in the peace within.

The *Hong-Sau mantra* is not a specific for banishing pain. I show how it can be used for that purpose in order to clarify the point that interiorization of the mind must be practiced in daily life also, if we are to succeed in attaining interiorization in meditation.

What I've really given you, however, is a wonderful technique for developing concentration in meditation. The purpose of the technique is, as I said, to help you to interiorize the mind. Its more fundamental purpose is to help you to rise above body-consciousness altogether, by stilling the breath.

HONG-SAU AS A TECHNIQUE FOR MEDITATION

Sit upright in meditation. Tense and relax the body, as I taught you in earlier chapters. Relax the body deeply. Then relax your thoughts and emotions.

To begin the technique, first inhale deeply, then slowly exhale. Wait for the breath to come in of its own accord. Follow it mentally with the word *Hong*.

As the breath flows out, watch it, and mentally follow it with the word *Sau*.

Remember, this is not a breathing exercise. Don't inhale and exhale deliberately. Simply *watch* the breath.

Don't watch your body breathing. Watch the breath itself. Identify the breath with the *mantra Hong-Sau*.

Be particularly aware of the rest points between the breaths. Enjoy the peace, and the feeling of inward release and freedom that you feel when your body is without breath.

Practice this technique as long as you feel to. As a boy, Paramhansa Yogananda used to practice it for hours at a time, withdrawing ever more deeply into the spine until he found himself without breath altogether. He had ascended into soul-consciousness, where the physical functions were suspended and a higher reality took over that freed the soul for a time from bodily imperatives.

You may, if you like, chant *Hong-Sau* first at the medulla, dissolving ego-consciousness into inner peace. After a time, as you become more interiorized, concentrate at the Spiritual Eye between the eyebrows; feel the ego only in its relationship to soul-consciousness. Indeed, concentrating at the point between the eyebrows brings the awareness closer to the upper part of the nasal passage, where the breath enters the body. To center the awareness here makes it easier to watch the breath, and at the same time bring it into harmony with spiritual awareness.

With spiritual enlightenment, the chant *Hong-Sau* becomes transformed into the *mantra So Ham*: "I am He" becomes transformed into the realization "He is I; He is my true Self." Paramhansa Yogananda explained that an unenlightened human being performs every action from the center of ego-consciousness, in the medulla. An enlightened master, on the contrary, performs all his actions from a center of soul-consciousness, in the Spiritual Eye.

Hong-Sau will help you to convert ego-consciousness into the complete awareness of who and what you truly are: a manifestation of Pure Consciousness.

****

MEDITATION EXERCISE

To practice interiorization of the mind during normal waking consciousness, try this walking meditation. Walk alone, if possible, during this exercise, for its purpose is to interiorize the mind, not to externalize it in the company of others. At the same time, I am aware that walking meditations are often practiced in a group. Such practice has the advantage of formalizing one's practices; it can make you regular in them. So take it, if you like, as my personal preference. To me, this practice is too intimate for anything but solitary practice.

Throughout this practice, make it a point to relate to God, to God through Nature, and to your own higher Self.

Don't walk vigorously. In other words, don't hike. Walk easefully. Express in outward action the peace you feel in meditation.

Now, be aware of the energy as it moves through your body. Feel yourself surrounded by a great, inverted vortex of cosmic energy, spinning slowly around you, and drawing you upward toward its source in infinity.

Bring that energy down, after a time, into an awareness of its manifestation in your physical environment.

Listen to the birds singing: Hear the Divine Consciousness singing through them. Ask the Divine Mother if She hasn't some special message, in their singing, for you.

Listen to the sounds in your vicinity: to dogs barking, people's voices in the distance, cars moving. Feel the Divine Mother communicating with you through all those sounds.

Gaze at the sunlight as it trembles on a leaf; at the clouds sailing overhead; at the trees, the bushes; at countless objects around you. Share those visual impressions with the Divine Mother, as if also with your higher Self.

Feel the wind on your skin, the warmth of the sunlight or the coolness of the evening air. In every thought, in every impression, make the Divine Mother a participant.

If thoughts come to you in the form of words, share them with the Divine Mother as though you were talking *to* Her. Don't only think *about* Her, in the third person. Talk *to* Her.

Feel yourself as the breath of divine love and joy. Walk joyfully on an earth where all beings rejoice in their unseen, heavenly origin.

Chapter Sixteen

THE HIGHER STAGES

True meditation begins only after the mind has been interiorized. Up to that point the meditator is preparing himself, only, to make the assault on the interior city.

It may seem odd to apply such military images to a process so utterly non-violent. It isn't a military assault we're talking about, after all, but the final thrust of the soul toward Self-realization. And yet, we do in a sense have to assemble invading forces. There is a definite similarity between the spiritual path and a military campaign. Military analogies are apt not for the aggressiveness they may suggest, but for the fact that it takes a heroic effort to lift the mind out of the comfortable delusions of a lifetime—indeed, of many lifetimes.

Life's outer stages are precursors, in the process of human development, to the stages of inner progress. Spiritual seekers, too, fall into four categories: the *sudra* (peasant), *vaisya* (merchant), *kshatriya* (warrior), and *brahmin* (priest, or sage).

The *sudra* type of devotee procrastinates, saying, "When I am not so busy," or, "When these guests leave," or, "When I feel better: *then* I will meditate."

The *vaisya* type equates effort with results, or with "acquiring merit." Whether those results are sought in the form of spiritual experiences, of material abundance, or of good karma, there is in all such seeking an element of bargaining.

The *kshatriya* type is the strong-willed devotee who surrenders everything to God, who doesn't think in terms of rewards, but who offers up his ego and his very life in the struggle for self-conquest.

The *brahmin* type is one who has won the war at last. Such a one is eternally at rest in himself. For him, the need ceases for warlike images—citadels, weapons, invading armies, the push for victory. Defensive walls have been pulled down, and contented mind-citizens stroll about peacefully. Fields flourish with luxuriant herbs, and birds sing without fear of the hunter's bullet. Gone, now, is the need for the hero's valiant stance. The "enemy," always, was no outer foe: It was his own ego that had stood in the way of victory.

What the devotee "warrior" soon discovers is that it isn't any divine fortress that must be conquered, but the forces of his own delusion standing at the gates of his own city to prevent him from leaving it.

The warrior image takes on special meaning at this point. For Satan—the delusive tempter in every one of us—is not in any way a gentleman. He doesn't play by anything remotely resembling the Marquis of Queensberry rules. If he can trick us by fair means or foul (he inclines toward the foul), he won't hesitate. If your aim is to know the Truth, you will have to reach the point where no clever feint on his part can ever fool you again.

You won't win that struggle by throwing ink pots at him, as Martin Luther did (the stain is still there on the wall for visitors to see). You will have to use weapons of truth, honor, divine firmness, and great courage. But you will have to accept that it is a struggle to the death. You can't safely give the old man even a damp mattress in the barn to sleep on. He'll slip into the house at night and murder you in your sleep.

There are many occasions when compassion and leniency are sterling virtues. In the contest with your lower nature, however, they are the ultimate ploy of delusion. "Be kind to me," delusion cries. "Have you no heart?" The *Bhagavad Gita* tells us, "Resist that false, soft tenderness which saps the youthful vigor of the soul."

That entire scripture is set on a battlefield to underscore the true nature of the struggle for enlightenment.

Once your inner army has been assembled for its assault in full earnest on the City of God, remember, it isn't God you're battling. God is on your side! Deep, devotional meditation on Him will give you the strength and wisdom you need to win the war.

In the *Mahabharata,* the long epic from which the *Bhagavad Gita* is excerpted, Sri Krishna (representing God in inner converse with the soul), offers an alternative to the protagonists in a war, Arjuna and Duryodhana.* "Choose," he says, "between me on one side, and my army on the other. If your choice is me, I will be with you in battle, but I will take no personal part in the

---

*Arjuna in this timeless spiritual allegory represents the spiritual seeker. Duryodhana, ruler of the opposing army, represents material desire.

struggle. If your choice is my army, you will have a vast force fighting on your side, but you will not have me."

Arjuna, given first choice, replies, "I choose Thee, Lord. For where Thou art, there alone is victory." Duryodhana, on the other hand, is delighted to get the support of Krishna's entire army. It is Arjuna, of course, who wins the war.

Once the mind is interiorized, it can concentrate wholeheartedly on storming the gates. The important thing, now, is to become ever more deeply absorbed in superconsciousness.

Superconsciousness—by which I mean that aspect of Cosmic Mind which has entered outward manifestation—contains eight attributes: Light, Sound, Love, Wisdom, Power, Bliss, Peace, and Calmness.

Peace differs from calmness in one important respect: It is soothing and restful, a deeply enjoyable state after the mind's long, arduous struggle. Calmness, on the other hand, is dynamic. It is strong sunlight, as opposed to cleansing rain.

The eight attributes rarely, if ever, appear all at once. They resemble, rather, the facets of a diamond. Each is presented at the right moment, and to the right person. Meditators usually feel themselves attracted to one attribute or another, and are therefore more likely to experience that attribute in themselves. The higher stages of meditation entail progressively deeper absorption in one attribute or another of superconsciousness, until the soul expands to become all of them.

THE SIXTH STAGE:
DHARANA, THE FIRST PERCEPTION

It is important to realize that the experiences of higher meditation are in no way mind-born. They are *received,* that is, not created. Once the mind is interiorized, it becomes like an upturned crystal chalice, ready for filling. Calm, interiorized, and uplifted, it receives the first clear intimations of the ecstasies that await it in superconsciousness.

I don't mean that the meditator is vouchsafed no spiritual experiences before he reaches the sixth stage of meditation. Inner sounds and lights, tear-inducing love and joy, healing peace—all of these and more are enjoyed by many meditators from the very beginning. To perceive them clearly and steadily, however, instead of in fleeting glimpses, is another matter.

The moon, reflected in a lake's surface, rarely appears as it does in the sky. What is seen are reflections, leaping, glimmering, darting here and there in a thousand ripples, its light ever lacking in definition. Only when the surface of the lake is completely calm are the reflections in it perfectly clear. When that happens, one might almost be seeing the moon itself.

Dharana, the sixth stage, means "concentration." This concentration implies not only a focused mind: It implies the rippleless first stages of superconsciousness, when the ego perceives clearly at last levels of reality of which it has received only flickering glimpses before.

At this stage, even the thought "I am concentrating" is a distraction, and betrays an imperfection in one's mental focus.

THE EGO'S POSITIVE ASPECT

A word here about the ego, which receives many brickbats and few roses from those whose job it is to explain these spiritual teachings. Granted, the ego stands in the way of spiritual progress. Indeed, ego-consciousness is the cause of all our spiritual diseases: pride, selfishness, aggression, and—more negatively still—self-doubt, insecurity, and fear. But it is easy to forget that there is good and bad in everything.

The three *gunas*, or qualities, coexist at all levels of creation. Although the ego must be vanquished in the end, to make room for superconsciousness, it is also our egos that make it possible for us to attain superconsciousness, and the highest levels of refinement available to human nature. To say deprecatingly of anyone, "Oh, that's just his ego," is to invite the response from anyone who understands these things, "Well, *of course* it's his ego! What else could it be?"

The cure for ego-consciousness is not self-suppression. It is to use our self-awareness as an incentive to self-expansion, not to personal power and pride.

The ego is like the gravitational field of a planet, which is used by space probes to give them the additional power they need to extend their voyages into outer space. The ego magnetizes a thought or an inspiration by spinning it around the consciousness of "I," that it may pass on further toward the Spiritual Eye, and superconsciousness.

The ego also, however, can block the flow of creativity and inspiration by crying, "Wait a minute! The credit is all *mine*." In this case, the simile that comes to mind is a rubber tube such as one sees in a science laboratory. If the tube is squeezed tightly at any point, the substance or liquid passing through it may swell the tube and even burst it. This simile is actually suggested in common parlance, by the description of egotists as people with "swollen heads."

To keep the tube from bursting, one can either release one's pressure on it, or turn off the flow at the faucet. In the case of human beings, one can either release the pressure on the medulla by relaxing the thought of "I," or send less energy up to the brain. To release the pressure, we must stop taking personal credit for what we do, that our creative energy may continue flowing toward its natural destination in the Spiritual Eye. The way to send less energy up to the brain is to keep it engrossed in physical pleasures and satisfactions, to accept apathy as a normal mental condition, and to convince oneself that mediocrity is a normal state of being.

Many people who denounce ego in others (never in themselves!) seem to be suggesting that mediocrity is a sensible alternative to high aspiration. It is the solution delusion itself proposes: Lower your energy output; you'll be more comfortable if you avoid life's challenges.

It is interesting, incidentally, to note that bowing is the universal gesture of humility. To bow to others, or to God, releases tension in the medulla, and enables the energy to flow onward to the positive pole of the medulla, at the point between the eyebrows.

THE DISSOLUTION OF THE EGO

In the stage of *dharana,* ego is still present. Ego can't be merely affirmed into non-existence, any more than a flying bird can affirm the non-existence of air. From where else would a person begin his spiritual journey, if not from his human sense of self, which is the ego?

When the ego reaches the stage of *dharana,* it beholds, in a state of exaltation, that lofty Truth towards which it has so long aspired. Clearly, now, it sees the inner light, or hears the inner sounds. Yet it is still separated from these experiences by the thought, "I, this human being, am enjoying this experience."

THE SEVENTH STAGE: *DHYANA*

The seventh stage on the path is called *dhyana,* or "meditation." The reason I use the Sanskrit term here, instead of the English, is not because it contains subtle connotations the English misses, but because it *excludes* connotations that are suggested by the English.

For the word "meditation" embraces all the practices in this book. *Dhyana,* on the other hand, refers only to this particular stage on the path of meditation. *Dhyana* signifies that stage when the mind, calm and fully receptive, loses itself in the light (or in some other divine attribute) and finds its ego-consciousness dissolving in that light. If one is communing with *AUM,* the sound vibration is experienced in the entire body. The soul marvels in the realization: "*This* is what I am! Not a physical body, but a blissful manifestation of *AUM*."

The light that one beholds in deep meditation, or the sound that one hears, or the love or the joy, redefine one's self-awareness. One recognizes oneself as a manifestation of Infinite Truth, and longs to become absorbed in it.

Spiritual awakening is an "unlearning," finally, in the sense of being a process of divine remembering. "Ah, *yes!*" the soul murmurs. "I recall everything now. This is what I *am!*"

Dhyana, the seventh stage, is the true state of meditation. At this point the ego, contemplating the supernal reality, forgets its separate identity and *becomes* the soul.

THE EIGHTH STAGE: *SAMADHI*

At this point, spiritual progress becomes a matter of progressively deeper Self-remembrance. The soul, recalling its true nature, identifies itself more and more fully with that divine memory. It realizes itself, first, as only a projection of Pure Consciousness. Then, finally, it realizes itself as, in fact, Pure Consciousness.

Samadhi (oneness), the eighth and final stage on the meditative journey, comes when the soul, losing body-identity altogether, merges in the greater reality of which the body and everything else in creation is only a manifestation. The identity it abandons is not its physical body only, but its subtler bodies as well. Once that subtlest wall of separation is demolished, there is nothing to prevent it from merging into the Infinite. The wave, having played on the surface of the sea for many lives, merges back again into the sea—its motion dissolved at last in perfect stillness.

Samadhi is not a state of mind. It is cosmic consciousness, the state where the soul perceives itself as truly "center everywhere, circumference nowhere." In that state, no ripple on the sea of consciousness remains. Thoughts and feelings are completely stilled. This emptiness is the state of *nirvana*. The soul, in that emptiness, knows only that it exists. It is stripped to its ultimate, irreducible essence: the stark realization, "I AM."

This is not, however, the final state. It is a release: It is not final attainment. Into this emptiness then bursts a new reality: Bliss absolute; Love eternal. From knowing nothing but its self-existence, the soul discovers that it knows everything. From stripping the onion of its last peel—the last *kosha* covering the heart—the soul proceeds to discover that it *is* everything. In possessing nothing, it finds that it possesses everything. It is *Satchidananda:* ever-existing, ever-conscious, ever-*new* Bliss.

There are several stages of *samadhi.* To attain divine perfection, not only must the ego transcend itself in soul-consciousness: The soul must convince itself that it truly *is* free in Infinity.

Those who imagine that God seeks to impose a state of ego-lessness on the soul have little idea of how completely we must persuade Him that we long for Him alone.

At first, the ego's addiction to a separate existence allows the soul only brief flights of ecstasy before self-hood reasserts itself. The bird, imprisoned for eons in its little cage, fears to come out even though the door of the cage stands wide open. After a time, deciding that no threat is posed by that openness, the bird hops briefly outside—two or three hops, only—fluffs its wings, then hops hurriedly back to the reassurance of its cage again. Again it hops out, and ever and again returns, still preferring its delusive security to freedom. Then at last it begins to think, "Why, outside the cage is where I really belong!" At last, taking courage, it leaves its cage altogether, and flies out the window to embrace the freedom it had so long denied.

Different terms are used by saints of East and West to describe the final stages of liberation. Paramhansa Yogananda used the terms *sabikalpa samadhi* and *nirbikalpa samadhi.*

Sabikalpa samadhi, he said, describes that stage in which the soul first emerges from its ego-cage and merges in the cosmic light or sound (or into any of the other six aspects of divine consciousness). *Sabikalpa samadhi* is temporary, not permanent, oneness. The soul knows freedom in that state, but the memory of ego-bondage lingers, and pleads as if from the back of a deep cave, "Enjoy your Self for a time if you must: but please, remember me!"

Repeated sorties from the ego are required before the soul can retain its divine state of awareness even after it returns to outer consciousness. At this point it is no longer aware of the ego in human terms, but knows it as a manifestation of the infinite reality. In this state, it finally is able to retain its consciousness of inner freedom even while performing its normal human functions in this world. This, finally, is the state of *jivanmukta,* a state of eternal freedom because the soul is released from bondage to its former consciousness of "I" and "mine." This highest *samadhi* Paramhansa Yogananda termed *nirbikalpa samadhi.* Other great teachers have named it variously—*sahaja samadhi,* for example: "effortless *samadhi.*"

Nirbikalpa samadhi does not yet represent final emancipation, because the soul is still not free from all past karma. Final emancipation is attained when all the old seeds of karma have been destroyed. This final state of emancipation was attained by Buddha, Jesus Christ, Krishna, and others, including several great masters of modern times. Other masters are not less in the state of their realization, but only in that they have some past karma still to work out. Many such masters, my guru told me, keep some of their old karma as a way of drawing them back to help their disciples. For in that state, he explained, it doesn't matter when the old karma is destroyed. What hurry is there, after all, once you've attained cosmic consciousness? In *nirbikalpa* there is no longer any danger of slipping down the ladder, through succumbing to nostalgia for the little self. The ego no longer exists. There is only its remembered reality of many incarnations. Long-buried impressions still need persuading that they, too, were parts of a divine play— God alone dreaming the entire sequence: butcher, baker, and candlestick maker.

Only when the soul is convinced down to its last layer of consciousness that it is free, is final liberation attained.

Many people, somewhat aware of the Indian teachings, are familiar with the term *avatar*. Few people, however, even in India, understand it except superficially. *Avatar* means "divine descent into the material realm." An *avatar* is one who, having attained final liberation, returns to this world out of compassion to help all humanity to fulfill its spiritual destiny. An *avatar*, as distinct from lesser saints and masters, has a universal mission. He (or she) also has the power to bring as many souls to freedom as come for guidance and enlightenment. His power is no longer circumscribed. Like the power of God Himself, it is infinite.

Oneness, then, is the final goal of meditation. Well before that ultimate goal, however, one reaches the point where meditation is no longer needed as a formal practice, for every moment of one's life, every flicker of human consciousness, every atom of one's body is permeated throughout with divine bliss.

NARADA AND VISHNU

The Indian scriptures relate a story that allegorically describes the illusory nature of human existence.

The sage Narada, after many years of meditation, was blessed with the vision of God in human form as Vishnu, Preserver of the universe. Vishnu said to him, "Narada, ask of me any boon."

Narada replied, "I see so clearly now, Lord, that you are the sole reality in the universe. Help me to understand that power of delusion which keeps humanity roaming in spiritual ignorance for so many countless incarnations."

Vishnu said, "Come, Narada. Let us take a walk."

After proceeding for some distance, they came upon a vast, sandy waste. Crossing it, they beheld at last a village in the distance.

"Narada," said Vishnu, "I'm very thirsty. Won't you please go to that village and fetch me a drink of water?"

"Instantly, Lord!" Narada went to the village and knocked on the door of the first house he came to. A young woman opened the door. To his amazement, there was instant recognition between them. Entering the house, Narada was welcomed by the girl's family. In time, the two were married and set up house in the village.

Narada started a little business. Two children were later born. The family was very happy. Twelve years passed, and a third child was born. Then, suddenly, a terrible storm struck, causing a flood. Their place of business, their home, their belongings—all were destroyed. Only the family was left intact.

As the flood waters rose all around them, they set off together in desperate search of high ground. Narada held one child with each hand, and balanced the baby on one shoulder.

They were struggling along valiantly, when his foot struck a submerged rock. He stumbled. Just then the baby slipped from his shoulder and was swept away in the swirling waters. Desperate to save the baby, he released the other two children and grasped at it. At that point, the other two were swept away also by the flood. His wife, overcome emotionally, lost her footing, too, and was swept away.

All was lost! Narada, losing heart, allowed himself to be carried off as well. Sinking into the raging current, he lost consciousness.

Some time later—how long? He knew not!—he awoke. Was he still alive? Had he awakened in some other world? Gazing about him, he saw all around him a vast stretch of brown water. Evidently he'd been swept to higher ground. Recalling the magnitude of his loss, he began quietly to weep.

Just then, a voice called him.

"Narada?" Anciently familiar that voice seemed.

"Narada?" again the voice called. Suddenly Narada realized that it wasn't muddy water that surrounded him, but endless stretches of brown sand.

He looked up. To his amazement, Vishnu stood there.

"Narada?" Vishnu addressed him for the third time. "What is this? Half an hour ago I sent you for a drink of water. Now I find you here, sleeping on the sand."

****

Meditation on the Moonrise

I wrote and recorded this visualization many years ago, with sitar accompaniment.* Because of the length

---

*The recording is available from Clarity Sound & Light, 14618 Tyler-Foote Road, Nevada City, CA 95959 (tel. 800-424-1055). It is entitled *Meditations to Awaken Superconsciousness: Guided Meditations on the Light.*

of this meditation, you may find it easier to follow in a recording.

It is evening.
Mentally watch the moonrise on a boundless lake.
Ripples lap against ripples
In endless counterpoint of restless rhythms.
Now here, now there—see, a few crests have joined,
And the ripples proudly swell, becoming waves.
But how fleeting their pride!
Watch: See how the waves reach upward,
But soon dip to form humble troughs!
Bobbing, the waters tell us:
"All is change."

Bright moonshapes dance upon the water.
Like laughing children
They run gaily on a lambent ripple,
Or pause breathlessly, in shining triumph
On a wave crest,
Ere sinking again in darkness
To wait for new life on another rise.
Here, too, the fickle moon-shapes say:
"All is change."

Now see your mind contained
In these boundless, dark waters.
The surface ripples are your restless thoughts—
Conscious and subconscious—
Your emotions and feelings,

Dancing, playing,
Rising hopefully,
Or sinking in discouragement,
Proud one minute,
Humbled the next.
Here, too, the waters tell you:
"All is change."

   But the moonlight above,
Caught imperfectly on the water's surface,
Remains ever calm, serene, unchanging.
This is the light of Spirit.
We reflect it so fleetingly, so distortedly,
In our restless minds!

   Now feel that the calm sky
Has formed a single, radiant drop
Of liquid peace.
This drop falls, striking the water.
Ripples of peace spread outward in all directions,
Soothing the dancing rhythm of your thoughts.
Wave on wave of peace spreads over you
Until, slowly, your mind reveals not a ripple.
Far, far out into the boundless night
No quiver of movement to disturb your calm!
And everywhere the moonlight on the water shines—
Almost as motionless as in the sky above.

   Gaze upward;
Release your mind from its watery heaviness.
You are now the sky!

229

Moon-rays of your peace spread quietly over the
    heavens,
Their calm light reaching out to infinity.
You have no boundaries,
No physical or mental weight,
No need to worry, to struggle and compete.
You are the endless sky!
With the cool moonbeams of your calmness
You have claimed the universe, and made it your own.
You and the endless light divine
Are One at last!

Chapter Seventeen

MEDITATION KEYS

How long should you meditate? The first rule is, Don't be ruled by what others do. What works well for them may not work for you. Accept that in certain ways you are unique. Here are a few general guidelines:

Intensity of effort is far more important than the time spent in meditation.

Never meditate to the point of mental fatigue, strain, or boredom. Enjoy what you do. Enjoy every aspect of your life—not an easy thing to do if one thinks about the aspects individually, but not so difficult if you concentrate on enjoying the inner Self. If you feel joy in meditation, stop meditating when the joy begins to diminish. One rule for right eating is to leave the table a little hungry. Apply this rule to meditation. In that way, you'll always look forward to your next time for meditation.

On the other hand, make an effort to meditate a little longer at least once a week. Four to six hours, even, is not exaggerated. And once a week won't kill you! Gradually you'll break the habit of thinking you can meditate only for short periods.

In longer meditations, imitate the ocean tides in their ebb and flow. Let periods of intense concentration alternate with periods of relaxed effort and peaceful receptivity. Like waves coming in to shore, high intensity will alternate with low intensity in long meditations, and there may be pauses when no waves come at all. Until you can transcend body-consciousness in superconsciousness, it is unlikely you'll be able to meditate deeply for very long. Think of your thoughts as dirt that has been stirred up in a glass. Stop stirring it, and it will gradually settle.

The greatest difficulty, in long meditations especially, is physical tension. Make an extra effort to keep your whole body relaxed, by following the relaxation methods taught in this book.

As a general guideline, I suggest you try to meditate at least half an hour twice a day—in the morning after you get up, and in the evening before going to bed. An hour and a half twice a day is better. But if you are a beginning meditator, more than one hour a day may be extreme. It is better to meditate a few minutes with deep concentration than a whole hour absentmindedly. Moreover, I don't mind bargaining with you! For although five minutes, let's say, isn't much for anyone who has developed a taste for meditation, it may be all you feel you can spend in the beginning. So be it! Think of meditation, if you like, as daily spiritual hygiene. You brush your teeth, bathe, and brush your hair every day: Why not add to that routine five minutes of meditation?

You'll come to enjoy meditating, in time. Then you'll find yourself meditating longer because you want to, and not because someone is nagging you to do so. But if you think you're too busy, here's something to think about: You can always find the time for something you enjoy doing, can't you? In time, you'll wonder how you ever lived without meditating daily. And the answer, of course, will be: You didn't. What you did, that is, wasn't really living.

Be natural in your efforts. Make haste slowly, as the saying goes. Don't force yourself to meditate when you'd very much rather be doing something else.

At the same time, don't stop meditating altogether with the excuse that you have other things to do. Remember, there's only one direction to go that makes any lasting sense: toward your own Self, in superconsciousness. No substitute will ever work for you; it's never worked for anyone. No appointment is more important than your appointment with—not death: *life*.

Be *a little* stern with yourself. Success won't come to people who never try. Only bear in mind that tension is counterproductive. In meditation, concentrate first of all on relaxation.

Remember this also: The more you meditate, the more you'll want to meditate; but the less you meditate, the less you'll enjoy doing it.

Another rule: As soon as you sit for meditation, get "down to business." Don't dawdle, as if telling yourself, "Oh, I have a whole hour, so what's the rush?"

Be regular in your hours and practices of meditation. Saying that reminds me of a typewriter I bought when I was seventeen. At the time I also bought an instruction manual that explained the touch system. For a week or two I practiced the exercises in the manual assiduously, mastering the system to the point where I finally learned to type quite rapidly. At that time, however, I was so eager to begin using the touch system that I ignored the exercises for learning the numerals. "I'll learn them," I told myself, "as I go along." The result? Today, more than fifty years later, I *still* need to look at the number keys when I want to use them.

So—be specific in your practices. Don't tell yourself they'll just sort themselves out someday by some process of osmosis.

It is a good practice to meditate at the same hours every day. Routine conditions the mind. You'll find yourself *wanting* to meditate whenever those hours return. It will be much easier, then, to set all distractions aside.

Stick to your routine as best as you can. To help you in creating one, here are a few suggestions:

1) Do the energization exercise in Chapter 10. If you learn this entire system of exercises, practice it daily— either before or after meditation. (Paramhansa Yogananda recommended doing them before.)

2) As soon as you sit to meditate, pray for depth and for guidance in your meditation. Pray also for peace for all humanity. Don't isolate your sympathies from others; embrace all in your divine love.

3) Chant and/or repeat affirmations, according to your personal predilection.

4) Tense and relax the whole body two or three times. Inhale before tensing, exhale with relaxation. This practice will help relax you mentally, as well as physically.

5) Expand your consciousness by following one of the visualization exercises in this book.

6) Practice *navi kriya.*

7) Practice *Hong-Sau* for a time—not less than half an hour, if possible.

8) After practicing the techniques, and for at least a quarter of your total meditation time, practice devotion, or listen to the inner sounds, or raise your energy from the heart center to the point between the eyebrows. Practice again one of the visualization exercises.

We develop intuition, Paramhansa Yogananda said, by prolonging the peaceful aftereffects of the meditation techniques.

After meditation, don't strip your mental gears by plunging hastily into outer activity. Try to carry the meditative peace into everything you do. To develop this habit, it may help to begin with outward activities that don't involve your mind too much. While doing them, chant inwardly to God. The walking meditation is an excellent practice for bridging the gap between meditative peace and outward busyness. If you can't devote time to walking calmly after meditation, try doing things slowly for a bit, consciously bringing peace and energy into your muscles and bodily movements.

As a focus for your devotion, you may find it helpful to set up an altar in your place of meditation. Include pictures on the altar, if you like, of saints, or of images of God, or of infinite light and space. (You may even find photographs of stars and galaxies helpful, as reminders of the vastness of space.)

A helpful practice also, if it pleases you, is the burning of incense as a devotional offering. The sense of smell is closely related to the memory faculty. You may recall, for example, catching in some fleeting scent a reminder of some childhood episode that awakened a host of associated memories. Incense, when used regularly in meditation, will help to create meditative associations in your mind, and bring you more quickly, therefore, to inner calmness.

Generally speaking, it is best to meditate in quiet places, and at quiet times of the day. It is also good occasionally, however, to discipline the mind. Don't pamper it. You may even like to meditate, sometimes, in noisy places, as a mental discipline. Don't sit where people will see you and wonder what you're doing. Or, if the place is public, don't sit in such a way as to call attention to yourself. In this case, you might practice looking ahead of you with open eyes.

One way of becoming virtually invisible in public is to put out the thought "I'm not here." Send no mental tendrils out to your environment. Rather, put out a vibration of non-being—somewhat along the principle of modern noise-cancellation technology, where sound waves are nullified by projecting sounds of an opposite wave pattern. Obliterate "people-consciousness" from your mind. You'll be surprised to how little an extent people notice you. Quite possibly they won't notice you at all: That is, they may see you, but they won't observe you.

Wait two or three hours, if possible, after a heavy meal before beginning meditation. If this delay is impossible,

236

however, or inconvenient, don't worry about it. Obstacles, if unavoidable, should be welcomed: They help to strengthen the will power.

Be more conscious of living in a world composed of energy and vibrations. Remind yourself always that you are not the body: You are consciousness working, through energy, to animate the body.

Above all in meditation, be happy! If you want to experience peace, meditate peacefully. If you want to know love, offer love first, yourself. It isn't that superconscious states can be created by right attitudes. They don't appear by command performance of the conscious mind, but are the fruits, rather, of right meditation. However, you can hold yourself in readiness for those experiences by placing yourself on their "wavelength," instead of clinging with "scientific objectivity" to opposite states of consciousness.

There are techniques of meditation that I might have included in this book. Strictures exist, however, which I honor, against making the techniques available too openly. I am happy to share with you as much teaching as you want from me, but where certain techniques are concerned I must be satisfied that, in your wanting, there is also deep earnestness. The more I am asked, the more also I'll be able to give. And where my own capacity fails, there are great masters behind me whose power is far greater than my own. But the asking must be right.

Initiation is important for the sincere seeker. If you want to explore these teachings more deeply, I invite you to write to The Expanding Light. But if you are satisfied with what is contained in these pages, then I, too, am satisfied.

The path to which God draws you is a sacred matter. It is between you and Him. For those who follow any path there should never be a spirit of rivalry; there should be mutual appreciation. I will never seek to influence you in these matters. My desire for you is simply this: that you find your own Self, within.

****

MEDITATION EXERCISE

Expansion of Light

Sit upright.
Sit very still.
Feel that, surrounding your body,
Is an infinity of dark space.
Listen intently:
Listen to the whispering silence!

Out of silence was sound born.
Out of darkness the light came.
Of that light, suns and galaxies drew their substance.
Light, not form, is the truth that infuses the universe.

Surround your body now with a halo of blue light—
Soft, soothing—a luminous peace.
Light enters you;
It pierces the pores of your skin;

Space lies outside you no longer: It has made you its
own.
It reaches deep into your muscles, your bones.
The sense of heaviness has been lifted from you.
You are made of pure light.

Like a boundless sphere, now,
The light has started to grow.
Shining freedom—claim it your own!
Light and joy thrill the air of the room.
The people, the objects nearby—
All these, in the peacefulness of that blue light and
joy,
Are one with you.

See: Light is embracing the house in which you
live.
It reaches out to your neighborhood—
To your township.
Like an expanding sail, ever outward
The light swells.
It embraces your country—
Your continent—
The world!
The whole world is basking
In the peaceful radiance of your joy.

Softly, now—
Release your light from the boundaries of this world.
Behold, light rays stream out
To the limits of the solar system—

To distant stars—
To our galactic fringe.
At last, countless galaxies in all space,
Their stars, tiny like the lights of a far-off city,
Glimmer serenely in the vastness of your being.

God's light and you are one!
God's joy and you are one!
O ray of the Infinite! You are not only this little body:
You are more—much more.
Boundless! Eternal!
All the atoms of creation gather,
Like thirsty children,
To drink from the waters,
To play in the fountain spray
Of your inexhaustible peace!

PART III

SUPERCONSCIOUS LIVING

Chapter Eighteen

INTUITIVE GUIDANCE

You will attain superconsciousness more quickly if you seek to attune yourself with it in your daily activities, and not only in meditation. The more you seek to be guided by intuition, which is an aspect of superconsciousness, the greater success you will meet in every undertaking. For the rational mind can only point to probable solutions. Intuition, rooted as it is in superconsciousness, will supply you with clear answers.

From a superconscious perspective, all life is a unity. From a rational perspective, life is *dis*unity—a bewildering jigsaw puzzle, often, with many pieces that never seem to belong together.

With the constant increase of information nowadays, knowledge is becoming so complex that no one really knows how to process it anymore. Even with such aids as computers and databases, people are overwhelmed by all the new facts bombarding them. They wonder if they can retain control of their lives, when the sheer flood of information is sweeping their little boats into a whirlpool. Rapidly losing sight of their moral convictions, they no longer seriously believe such a thing as wisdom exists.

The Greek Sophist Zeno presented an interesting paradox, which, whether he intended it so or not, illustrates the inadequacy of logic. An arrow's flight, he said, viewed at any point on its journey, is stationary. Since the arrow's flight consists of innumerable points, each of which is stationary, its movement is an illusion.

Zeno's error, of course, lay in trying to analyze that movement instead of viewing it as a phenomenon in itself. Analysis demands separation and categorization. It demands that what it studies be motionless that it may be analyzed further. Logic is like a sentry, commanding life: "*Stand,* and deliver."

One problem with logic is that if the premise is wrong, the syllogism will be wrong also. Zeno's premise was that those imaginary points were stationary. He imagined them that way because it is the way of logic itself to "freeze" reality in still poses.

The Greeks were, as far as we know, the first of our Western breed of rationalists. Zeno, of course, may only have been showing the absurdity of trying to understand things by seeing them as numerous non-functioning parts—by analyzing motion into motionlessness, and freezing living forms into lifeless, but controllable, "exhibits." Herein lies the weakness of logic. The intellect, with its analytical tendency, is more naturally attuned to static than to living realities. Logic finds difficulty in seeing unity everywhere—in seeing life as a flow, and the universe as living and conscious. The intellect, working from facts and definitions, cannot readily grasp the truth that the material universe is only the outer shell of life and consciousness.

But the intellect serves a valuable function. A unitive view of life, reined, but not motivated, by the intellect is the secret of creativity. Creativity, like life itself, comes with flowing awareness. It can only be channeled by intelligence. Intelligence, though useful, is subordinate to intuition. That is why creative people, relying too little on the intellect, are often not adept at analyzing their own work, or art in general. Professional critics, on the other hand, relying too much on the intellect, are not often creative themselves. For the highest creativity, a balance is needed between intellect and intuition.

To live superconsciously is to maximize our abilities in every department of life. For the rational mind, with its focus on differences, is essentially problem-oriented. The superconscious, with its broader, more unitive view, is solution-oriented.

The unitive view is justified objectively in Nature. Every natural problem has a corresponding solution. American Indians claim that wherever a poisonous plant grows, its antidote will be growing nearby.

In India I was told that in the tail of a cobra there exists an antidote to the snake's venom. This isn't a cure I'd care to verify, but my informant claimed that if a person is bitten by a cobra, he should bite hard on the tip of the cobra's tail and suck on its antivenom. This claim, valid or not, is certainly based on a valid principle.

Superconscious living means to trust one's life to the flow of a higher wisdom. Superconsciousness arranges things in ways that we might never imagine.

I've seen this principle at work on countless occasions. Always it has worked better than any solution I might have provided, myself.

Years ago, in India, I flew to Calcutta from New Delhi. Friends of mine had promised to meet me at Dum Dum Airport, but as things turned out they were delayed by heavy traffic and arrived much later. Meanwhile, finding myself at a loss as to what to do, I stood quietly for a moment and asked the Divine Mother, "What do You want?"

Now, I should mention that my one regret on coming to Calcutta had been that I'd been unable to locate the address of a friend of mine, a Dr. Misra, whom I'd known in America, where he'd been getting his Ph.D. Since then he'd returned to India, and was living in Bhubaneswar, some two or three hundred miles south of Calcutta. I'd been hoping to visit him during this time in India, but now it appeared I'd be unable to do so.

As I paused silently, offering up my predicament to God, there occurred a dramatic turn of events. An Indian gentleman on his way through the crowd toward the exit stopped and took a closer look at me. Then he addressed me, speaking in the manner of his country, "Please excuse me, sir, but what is your good name?" Surprised at the question, I answered him.

"Ah," he responded, delighted. "I thought you must be he! I recognized you from your photograph. A friend of mine, Dr. Misra, showed it to me after his return from America."

"Dr. Misra!" I exclaimed in astonishment. "If it's the Dr. Misra I'm thinking of, he lives in Bhubaneswar."

"It is just of him that I am speaking. As I say, I recognized you from the photograph he took of you."

"Why, I've been hoping I could see him! Would you be so kind as to give me his address?"

"There is no need to see him in Bhubaneswar," the gentleman replied. "Dr. Misra is visiting Calcutta just now. I've flown here just for the purpose of meeting him myself. Let me take you to him."

And so I was able to see my friend, who also put me up for the night. (A fortunate extra bonus, as it turned out. I learned later that all the hotels had been fully booked that night.)

My other friends, whom I'd tried unsuccessfully to contact from the airport, arrived long after my departure. We got together later, and my original program was soon "back on track" again.

Now, just think what would have happened had I reacted as most people would have to such a situation. They'd have dashed about asking questions, making telephone calls, stirring up a maximum of confusion, and, at last, taking a taxi to a succession of fully booked hotels. My brief pause to put matters in God's hands solved my entire dilemma.

I can imagine the analytical mind objecting, "Well, what if that man hadn't been there? It was only a coincidence that he happened to arrive in Calcutta just then, and that he happened to notice you. His agenda was a different one altogether, and had nothing to do with meeting you." My answer would be that, if that man hadn't happened to come by, something else would have happened. And even if nothing had happened, I'd still have been in a better frame of mind to handle the situation than I would have, had I succumbed to worry and confusion.

What I've learned in life is that, if you place matters *with complete trust* in God's hands, things always work out for the best. Sometimes all you gain is the calmness to make the best of what might otherwise seem a bad situation. That does happen, for many of life's problems are "solved" by simply changing our outlook. Often, however, the change is objective also. Events turn out so amazingly well that people later refer to them as miraculous. And yet it isn't really a question of miracles. It is simply that this is how the superconscious works: It ties things together. It dissolves difficulties. It offers practical solutions, where the rational mind sees nothing but problems.

Where people see disunity, the superconscious mind sees the expression of Oneness in everything. To superconsciousness, everything is related. Not relative, merely: *related*. You don't have to be in superconsciousness to *think* superconsciously. All you have to do is train your mind to adjust your thinking to superconscious modes of perception.

Think more unitively, less analytically. Concentrate on finding the relationships between things; don't dwell at length on the differences. See others as your own greater Self. They are not alien to you. Look on them as friends, even if they appear outwardly to be strangers.

Years ago, I received a beautiful demonstration of the practical merits of this unitive view. It was in Paris,

France, and—as it happened—on my birthday. I wanted to attend a concert as a birthday present to myself.

I arrived at the church where the concert was to be held, but found about fifty people being turned away by an official, with the explanation that there was no room left.

"Mais c'est mon anniversaire!" I cried out ("But it's my birthday!"). I couldn't believe I'd be disappointed on this special occasion.

"Alors, monsieur, bon anniversaire! Entrez, s'il vous plaît," he replied ("Well in that case, sir, happy birthday! Please come in."). He opened the door for me.

The main seating area was completely filled, so I was given a seat on a folding chair behind the altar, where a handful of others were seated already. We faced an audience, on the other side of us from the orchestra, of about seven hundred people.

It was a joy-filled occasion. In addition to the beauty of the music, I felt a sense of expansive love for everyone present.

Later, on the Métro (the French subway), an old woman approached me. "Don't you remember me?" she inquired. No, I said regretfully, I didn't. Surprised, she cried, "But I was in the audience in the church this evening!"

How could I have noticed her in that throng? But somehow she'd felt a connection with me. She went on to confide in me a problem she was having with her daughter, as though I were a close friend of the family.

See oneness everywhere, and the universe itself will respond to you in kind. Be solution-oriented, as I said, not problem-oriented. To do that, approach your problems with perfect confidence that their solution is already there, waiting to be found. The intellect will try to discourage such faith, whispering, "Caution! Common sense!" But I've found that strong faith brings better results than any I could have imagined, myself.

What is particularly needed is to give one's faith the motive force of will power and energy. Energy generates magnetism, which attracts the inspiration.

Can we really attract inspiration at will? Yes indeed! Strong energy, powered by confidence (which must be rooted in faith; it must not be *ego*-confidence) can attract inspirations, opportunities, solutions to problems—anything.

This is a delicate point for me to clarify, and for others to get clear. For instance, it isn't a question of wanting anything, personally, but of wanting it because it is *right*. It is important to exclude ego-motivation as much as possible. It's also important that faith not become an excuse for irresponsibility. To live superconsciously means to cooperate with the superconscious flow, not to expect that flow to do everything for you.

It's a question of energy *in cooperation with* faith. You must be wholly focused on whatever you are doing, without seeing yourself as the doer.

Many highly creative people rise to certain heights of creativity, then find it impossible to rise any farther. Why? Many of them actually begin, at a certain point, to lose their creativity. Again, why? Always, it seems to me, the loss follows an increase of egotism. Their thought "I'm doing it all myself" blocks the energy-flow to the superconscious, whence they derived their highest inspiration. The energy, then, blocked in the seat of ego in the medulla, is prevented from flowing on toward the seat of superconsciousness in the Spiritual Eye.

A number of artists, composers, and other creative people have even become mentally unbalanced—enough of them to inspire the popular saying that only a fine line divides genius from madness. Interestingly, this doesn't seem to have been so much the case prior to the Romantic Era. With the dawn of Romanticism, creative artists—in reaction, probably, to the "soullessness" of the industrial revolution—began to be praised for their "exquisite" sensibility.

Look at the nineteenth century. Why did so many artists—Hugo Wolf, Nietzsche, van Gogh, Scriabine, to name a few—lose their sanity? Many others, though not certifiably insane, gave every evidence of instability. Such imbalances don't seem to have been so much in evidence previously, when artistic creativity itself was rendered less homage. It is as though the high energy required to create a masterpiece, if that energy is blocked by a growing sense on the artist's part of his own importance in the scheme of things, resulted in disturbances to the brain.

If you are creating something, or even if you are seeking guidance in anything that you do, relax the consciousness in the medulla of personal "doership," and direct the flow of energy onward to the point between the eyebrows. Keep your thoughts uplifted while you work. Don't accept an initial inspiration, then snatch the ball from Higher Guidance and run with it yourself.

The melody of many a song, as just an example, begins with a beautiful first line, then rapidly loses inspiration. Such a song may achieve fame purely on the strength of its first line. How much lovelier it might have been, had the composer not tried to work out the rest of the melody in his mind, but instead continued to hold his energy up to superconsciousness for further guidance.

Don't let the labor involved in dealing with the mechanics of a creative work tempt you to relax your grip on superconsciousness.

Tuning In to Higher Guidance

Whenever you need special guidance but find none forthcoming, try following these suggestions:

1) Ask for guidance from superconsciousness at the Spiritual Eye.

2) Wait for a response in the heart center. Be completely impartial. Don't intrude your personal desires into this process. Pray, "Thy will, not mine, be done."

3) If no guidance comes, propose several alternative solutions at the Spiritual Eye. See if one of them receives special endorsement in the heart.

4) Guidance often comes only after an idea has been made concrete by setting it in motion. If, therefore, you receive no answer in meditation, act in whatever way seems reasonable to you, but continue to listen for guidance in the heart.

At a certain point, if your direction is right, you will feel the endorsement you've been seeking. But if your direction is wrong, suddenly you will *know* it is wrong. In that case, try something else, until the endorsement comes.

To refuse to act until you receive inner guidance is good only if you can keep your level of energy and expectation high. For it is high energy and high expectation that attract guidance. If you must act because you have no other way of maintaining that level of energy, then go ahead and act. Often, it is better to act, even in error, than not to act at all.

5) Even if you feel inner guidance, never presume on it. That guidance may tell you, metaphorically speaking, to go north, but if you cease listening you may not hear it when, at the next corner, it tells you to turn east.

6) A problem is half solved already once it is stated clearly. In seeking guidance, form a clear mental picture of what it is you need. Then hold that picture up to superconsciousness at the point between the eyebrows. People often struggle for a long time to find the inspiration they want. No time at all is needed: only sufficient mental clarity, and energy.

Never use the claim of inner guidance as an argument for convincing others to listen to you. The flow of superconsciousness is always humble, never boastful. It doesn't cooperate with attitudes that discourage others from seeking their own inner guidance. To tell a person, "This is what my intuition tells me, so this is what we must all do," is to say, in effect, "God will speak only through me, not through anyone else." Such an attitude sooner or later gets its comeuppance. The divine law does not endorse pride.

SUPERCONSCIOUS ATTITUDES

Every quality that flowers naturally in superconsciousness should be affirmed by the conscious mind, and transferred by the conscious mind to the subconscious. Divine joy, for example, is a fruit of deep meditation. A person of scientific bent might decide to test this truth with a "controlled" experiment. To prove the reality of superconscious joy, he might determine to be as grim as possible during meditation. But the way to attune yourself to divine joy is to hold a joyful attitude, even though the true experience of divine joy is—to use Paramhansa Yogananda's words in his poem "Samadhi"—"beyond imagination of expectancy."

If you're expecting someone to visit you, you won't wait for him in the basement. If you're expecting a phone call, you won't drown out the sound of the telephone by turning on the electric blender. If you keep a grim attitude during meditation, you won't be prepared for the experience of joy even if it comes to you. It won't be your grimness, so much, that prevents you from experiencing joy as your essentially anti-superconscious attitude of skepticism, your resistance to the inner flow.

Be joyful in meditation. Be peaceful. Bless all the world with your love. And, even walking down a city street, secretly send divine love and blessings to everyone you pass. You'll be surprised how many strangers will treat you as a friend.

References

For your convenience, here is the list of books, audios, music albums, and retreat facilities that are referenced in this book:

Affirmations for Self-Healing, by J. Donald Walters. Nevada City: Crystal Clarity, Publishers, 1992.

Ananda Yoga for Higher Awareness by J. Donald Walters. Nevada City: Crystal Clarity, Publishers, 1994.

Aum, Mantra of Eternity, chanted by Donald Walters. Nevada City: Clarity Sound & Light, 1997.

Autobiography of a Yogi, by Paramhansa Yogananda. Nevada City: Crystal Clarity, Publishers, 1995. [Reprint of the original Philosophical Library edition, 1946.]

Bhagavad Gita. There are many good translations of this book available through your local bookstore. Because each edition has its strengths and weaknesses, there is no one definitive edition to recommend.

Meditations to Awaken Superconsciousness: Guided Meditations on the Light, by J. Donald Walters. Nevada City: Crystal Clarity, Publishers, 2000.

Out of the Labyrinth: For Those Who Want to Believe, But Can't, by J. Donald Walters. Nevada City: Crystal Clarity, Publishers, 2000. [Forthcoming new edition of *Crises in Modern Thought*, revised edition, 1988.]

The Rubaiyat of Omar Khayyam Explained, by Paramhansa Yogananda, edited by J. Donald Walters. Nevada City: Crystal Clarity, Publishers, 1994.

Scientific Healing Affirmations, by Paramahansa Yogananda. Los Angeles: Self-Realization Fellowship, 1981.

Yoga Sutras of Patanjali. There are many good translations of this book available through your local bookstore. Because each edition has its strengths and weaknesses, there is no one definitive edition to recommend.

For more information about meditation, yoga, and spiritual retreats, please contact:

The Expanding Light
14618 Tyler-Foote Road
Nevada City, CA 95959-8599
Telephone: 800-346-5350 or 530-478-7518
Internet: www.expandinglight.org
E-mail: info@expandinglight.org

Index

abstinence, sexual. *See brahmacharya*

acceptance, 71–72, 102; of others, 101, 102. *See also* non-acceptance; self-acceptance; *titiksha*

action. *See karma yoga*

affirmations, 110–11, 185–88; for before meditation, 26–27; limitations of, 69

ahankara. See ego

ahimsa, non-violence, 59, 69–73, 80, 85

altar, setting up of, 235

Ananda Village, 149

Anandamoyee Ma, 21, 103–4, 195

anxiety, overcoming, 95–96

aparigraha. See non-acceptance

Arjuna, 215–16

asana, right posture, 26, 89–97

astral body, 128–29, 204–6

astral universe, 138–39, 140–41

attitude, right: for centering, 99–106; importance of, 64–82, 85

attunement, 24, 102–4, 237, 243, 254; meditation exercise for, 176

AUM, cosmic creative vibration, 87; absorption in, 181–82; meditation exercise for, 188; pronunciation of, 135n; three aspects of, 135–36n. *See also* sounds, inner; "Word"

Aurobindo, Sri, on the *Vedas,* 126n

austerity, 79, 80, 86

avatar, divine incarnation, 225

baptism, 78

battle, spiritual path as, 213–16. *See also* conflict between subconscious and superconscious; spine, as battlefield

Bhagavad Gita, 125n; quoted, 7, 19, 37, 52, 57, 58, 71, 125, 147, 215

bhakti yoga, path of devotion, 56–58, 59–60, 62–63

Bharati Krishna Tirtha, Swami, on the *Vedas,* 126n

Bible, quoted, 154, 163, 181

bigotry, 114–15

bliss. *See* joy; *satchidananda*

body consciousness, rising above, 54, 80, 110–11, 120–23, 146–48, 237. *See also asana;* relaxation, physical

Bose, J. C., 19

bowing, explained, 219–20

brahmacharya, self-control, 76–78, 80, 86

brahmin. See "priestly" type

brain, 15–17, 108

breath, watching. *See Hong-Sau*

breathlessness, 209, 210

buddhi. See intellect

Buddhism. *See* lumbar center, concentration at; *nirvana*

calmness, achieving, 53, 66, 94, 216, 217, 248; meditation exercise for, 53. *See also* restlessness, overcoming

"castes" of spiritual development, 32–36, 37–38, 213–14

causal universe, 138, 140–41

celibacy. *See brahmacharya*

center, finding one's, 22, 113–23; meditation exercise for, 123–24

"center everywhere, circumference nowhere," 22, 98–99, 101, 105–6, 120–21, 193–94, 222

ceremonies, limitations of, 78, 79

chakras, spinal centers, 132–33. *See also* heart center; lumbar center; medulla oblongata; *sahasrara;* Spiritual Eye

chanting, 107, 177–88

chitta. See feeling

Christ, Jesus, 163. *See also* Bible, quoted

cleanliness, 78–79, 80, 86

common sense, its importance in meditation, 43

concentration. *See dharana; Hong-Sau*

conflict between subconscious and superconscious, 28–32, 89–92, 100–101, 125–28, 213–16

confusion, 115n

About the Author

A meditator and spiritual teacher for over 50 years, J. Donald Walters is widely considered one of the foremost living experts on meditation, yoga, and spiritual practice.

Walters is the founder of Ananda, a worldwide network of spiritual communities based on the yoga practices and philosophy of the great Indian sage, Paramhansa Yogananda.

J. Donald Walters' books and music have sold over 2.5 million copies worldwide and are translated into 22 languages. His best-selling books include *Meditation for Starters, The Path, Affirmations for Self-Healing, Money Magnetism,* and the *Secrets* books series. Walters is also the founder of Ananda Yoga™ and The Expanding Light yoga and meditation retreat in Northern California, one of the best-known and most popular retreats in America.

Walters has composed over 300 pieces of music including *The Mystic Harp* and *Mystic Harp 2*, both performed by the famed Irish harpist Derek Bell of the Grammy Award–winning group, The Chieftains.

MEDITATIONS TO AWAKEN SUPERCONSCIOUSNESS
GUIDED MEDITATIONS ON THE LIGHT
J. Donald Walters
Audio, 40 minutes, 1 Cassette

Visualizations are powerful ways to focus the mind for meditation. Designed both for beginning and experienced meditators, *Meditations to Awaken Super-consciousness* provides easy, gentle guidance to help beginners quickly feel the benefits of meditation and experienced practitioners break through blocks and deepen their experience. Featuring two beautiful guided meditations as well as an introductory section to prepare you for meditation, this stunning collection of visualizations can be used either as a companion to the book *Awaken to Superconsciousness* or by itself. "Meditation on the Moonrise" is specifically designed to help calm the mind and locate the wellspring of inner peace. "Expansion of Light" is intended to gently guide you past the limits of body and ego consciousness into higher states of awareness, into the superconsciousness.

MUSIC TO AWAKEN SUPERCONSCIOUSNESS
EXPERIENCE INNER PEACE, INTUITIVE GUIDANCE,
AND GREATER AWARENESS
Donald Walters, instrumental & vocal, 65 minutes, CD/cassette

Designed as a musical embodiment of the principles and practices presented in the book *Awaken to*

Superconsciousness, this album can be used in conjunction with the book or by itself. Each of the instrumental selections on this lush compilation expresses a different aspect of superconsciousness, helping you more easily access higher states of awareness. They will help you find deep calmness, joy, and radiant health, and intuitively guide you toward self-transcendence. Flexibly designed instruction in the liner notes explains how you can actively use this recording to achieve superconscious awareness, or, if preferred, the music can be used simply as background music for relaxation and meditation, subtly drawing you upward toward states of calm, expansive joy.

Other titles available from
CRYSTAL CLARITY, PUBLISHERS

MEDITATION FOR STARTERS
J. Donald Walters
Trade Paperback, 136 pages

- ◆ Finalist—Best New Age Book—1997 Ben Franklin Award
- ◆ Finalist—Best Video—1999 Ben Franklin Award
- ◆ Finalist—Best Video—1999 Videographers Award
- ◆ One Spirit Book-of-the-Month Club Alternate Selection

"A gentle guide to entering the most majestic, fulfilling dimensions of consciousness. J. Donald Walters is a wise teacher whose words convey love and compassion. Read and listen and allow your life to change."
—Larry Dossey, M.D.,author of *Prayer Is Good Medicine*

"Gives both beginning and longtime meditators proven techniques and powerful visualizations to heighten contemplative experiences. Highly recommended."
—PJ Birosik, *New Age Music News & Reviews*

Meditation brings balance into our lives, providing an oasis of profound rest and renewal. Doctors are even prescribing it for a variety of stress-related diseases. This award-winning book offers simple but powerful guidelines for attaining inner peace. Learn to prepare the body and mind for meditation, special breathing techniques, ways to focus and "let go," develop superconscious awareness, sharpen your willpower, and increase intuition and calmness. *Meditation for Starters* is available as a book & CD set, book & cassette set, and as a 79-minute video. Each item is also sold separately.

Companion CD or cassette: Includes further instruction on meditation. In the first 30 minutes, learn the fundamentals of meditation plus step-by-step instruction. The second half contains a beautiful and deeply interiorizing visualization set to soothing music, entitled *Land of Mystery*.

sCompanion Video: This 79-minute video is divided into two parts. Part I includes a talk and instruction by Walters, interwoven with an enchanting guided visualization set to music. Part II is the entire *Land of Mystery* guided visualization without instruction.

SECRETS OF MEDITATION
J. Donald Walters
Hardcover, color photographs, 72 pages

Benjamin Franklin Award Winner!
Finalist—Best New Age Book

Full of inspiring, helpful tips on meditation, this little desktop guide offers a seed thought for every day of the month. It has been said that we are what we eat. It would be truer to say, "We are what we think." For our minds express, and also influence, the reality of what we are far more than our bodies do. *Secrets of Meditation* is a potent guide to meditation that points the way to the deeper levels of inner peace that we all seek. The book contains 31 daily affirmations to help you bring the essentials of meditation into your life. Beautiful color photographs accompany each affirmation.

THE PATH
One Man's Quest on the Only Path There Is
J. Donald Walters (Swami Kriyananda)
Trade paperback, 420 pages

What would it be like to live with a great spiritual master? Here, with over 400 stories and sayings of Paramhansa Yogananda, is the inspiring story of one man's search for truth. It led him to the great master's door, where he learned to live the spiritual life more perfectly through his teacher's training and example. A vitally useful guide for sincere seekers on any path. Filled with insightful stories and mystical adventures, *The Path* is considered by many as a companion to Yogananda's *Autobiography of a Yogi*.

AUTOBIOGRAPHY OF A YOGI
Paramhansa Yogananda
(Reprint of the Philosophical Library 1946 First Edition)
Trade Paperback, 481 pages with photographs

*"In the original edition, coming from the period of
Yogananda's life, one is more in contact with Yogananda himself. It is prior to the institutionalization that often follows
many great personalities once they have passed on. . . . While
Yogananda founded centers and organizations, his concern
was more with guiding individuals to direct communion
with Divinity rather than with promoting any one church as
opposed to another. This spirit is easier to grasp in the original edition of this great spiritual and yogic classic."*

—David Frawley, Director,
American Institute of Vedic Studies

*". . . an eyewitness recountal of the extraordinary lives
and powers of modern Hindu saints, the book has importance both timely and timeless."*

—W.Y. Evans-Wentz,
M.A., D.Litt., D.Sc., Jesus College, Oxford
Author of *The Tibetan Book of the Dead*

Followers of many religious traditions have come to recognize this book as a masterpiece of spiritual literature.
Yogananda was the first yoga master of India whose mission it was to live and teach in the West. His first-hand
account of his life experiences includes childhood reve-
lations, stories of his visits to saints and masters in
India, and long-secret teachings of Self-realization that
he made available to the Western reader. This highly
prized verbatim reprinting of the original 1946 edition
is the only one available free from textual changes made

after Yogananda's death. Experience all its inherent power, just as the great master of yoga first presented it.

THE HINDU WAY OF AWAKENING
ITS REVELATION, ITS SYMBOLS
AN ESSENTIAL VIEW OF RELIGION
Swami Kriyananda (J. Donald Walters)
Trade paperback, 352 pages

Swami Kriyananda's inspired, entertaining, energetic writing style makes this book delightful reading for anyone interested in spirituality and the deeper meanings of religion. A master of word imagery, he brings order to the seeming chaos of symbols and deities in Hinduism, revealing the underlying teachings from which they arise, truths inherent in all religions, and their essential purpose: the direct inner experience of God. Intended for followers of all faiths—and no faith—*The Hindu Way of Awakening* will enrich your life and feed your soul.

AFFIRMATIONS FOR SELF-HEALING
J. Donald Walters
Trade paperback, 126 pages

Our thoughts influence, to a great extent, our physical health. An affirmation is a statement of truth which one aspires to absorb into one's life. This book contains 52 affirmations and prayers devoted to strengthening qualities within ourselves such as will power, patience, good health, forgiveness, security, and happiness.

SURRENDER: MYSTICAL MUSIC FOR YOGA

Derek Bell & Agni instrumental, 58 minutes
CD/cassette

Famed harpist Derek Bell and composer Donald Walters, the team behind the best-selling albums *Mystic Harp* and *Mystic Harp 2*, now turn their attention to creating the most original and useful yoga recording available. Contoured to mirror the actual flow of real yoga classes, *Surrender* is a carefully crafted musical sequence created specifically for use during any style of hatha yoga session. Also featuring sitar player Agni, and including tabla, keyboards, and cello, this beautiful musical odyssey is a breathtaking companion for a yoga session or can simply be used as soothing background music.

THE MYSTIC HARP

Derek Bell instrumental, 70 minutes, CD/cassette

Original melodies by Donald Walters capture the mythical quality of traditional Celtic music. Derek plays Celtic harp on each of the nineteen richly orchestrated melodies and is joined on the New Dawn track by renowned violinist Alasdair Fraser.

". . . an ambiance quiet and dreamy enough to appeal to new age audiences and Celtic folkies."

—*Billboard* magazine

"Utterly radiant, with noble simplicity and innocence."
—*NAPRA Review*

MYSTIC HARP 2
Derek Bell instrumental, 72 minutes, CD/cassette

Derek Bell, the legendary harpist of the five time Grammy award–winning group The Chieftains, returns for the sequel to the best-selling album, *The Mystic Harp.* Here Derek once again displays his unparalleled artistry in twenty new melodies written by Donald Walters.

WINDOWS ON THE WORLD
Donald Walters vocal, 74 minutes, CD/cassette

Beautifully sung, global in scope, inspired by life in nine different countries, these twenty-two songs will touch the hearts of all who listen.

"A voice that enthralls, and a vision that ennobles."
—Dr. Haridas Chaudhuri
Founder of the California Institute of Integral Studies